The Accelerated Necromancer

Gavin Fox

Erebus Society

Erebus Society

First published in Great Britain in 2024
Erebus Society

First Edition

ISBN: 978-1-912461-60-8

www.ErebusSociety.com

Table of Contens

BOOK ONE

BOOK TWO

BOOK THREE

Preface

Magick is the journey, not the destination. I forget exactly where on the proto-internet I originally came across that unapologetic twist upon a much more well known phrase, but it stuck with me ever since. Like a clarion call to arms and excuse to work outside of the esoteric mainstream it empowered my already anarchic nature, giving the vulpine trickster within room to play.

The story that led me to first set foot upon this cemetery path is a long and twisting one, though that is not really important right now. This book is not about me, nor do I intend to bore you all with stories of recurring nightmares, lost loved ones and the Reaper's repeated kiss. Those occasionally painful memories, while no doubt interesting to some, risk obscuring the underlying message of this work.

No, I am just one adept among many, and I do not claim to be special by virtue of my ability to string words together on a page. Destiny, though, may have played a role in choosing someone who actually enjoys the process of writing as the vessel for what would eventually coalesce into a mostly stable blending of the nature, death and chaos currents, one already primed for ritualistic use right out of the box too.

I have long made it a point to try and help others avoid the same pitfalls I most definitely fell into along my own occult journey. That is not to say that some of those expected bruises are not a necessary part of the growth of the will of course. Some, yes, but not all, and the ones that are avoidable might as well be sidestepped.

So as a result I rather puckishly chose to adopt a variation on the Thelemic Powers of the Sphinx to guide my life from the point I started blogging about necromancy and chaos magick right through to today. 'To Know, To Dare, To Will, To Tell The Whole Damn World.' These are the tenets I stand and fall by. My reason to write. The need to share.

I have no delusions of mastery, nor do I desire disciples in the classic sense either. No. I am not a leader, just a fellow traveller towards the Veil who is offering you all a seat beside him on the graveyard bench while the echoes and shards of former lives drift quietly on by. I might even have a spare sandwich in my knapsack now I think about it.

So that's all I have to say then. Preface over. Just the book you hold in your hands now and the strength of those likely strange ideas. My work is done, and yours is just beginning. These words are my risen army, and by reading this you become a surrogate parent to that tattered offspring. Treat them well, fellow adept, and you will go far.

Gavin Fox

Cardiff, UK

Mabon 2024

Introduction

As a system accelerated necromancy synthesises and reconciles various different esoteric disciplines, each of which helps to give this stridently modern art its distinct shape. Most prominent among these are chaos magick, urban shamanism, left hand path spiritualism and of course modern witchcraft too. But the adaptation does not end there. Even the Otherworld that it weaves itself around is far from classical in tone.

From a literary point of view this text is something of an oddity. The basic idea was to create a handbook for practitioners of all experience levels, a workshop manual for the cemetery path. But try as I might the resulting list of witchy techniques and chaos magick mind hacks just failed to make sense without briefly including all the context and background which led me to adopt them in the first place.

Yes, there is much cosmology here, an honest representation of the system that I created over many long years of reading and ritual. But what I achieved I did mostly on my own. So the terminology used throughout may appear alien to some. Ghostform. Digital afterlife. Repeated nods back to Tiamat's womb and a many faced Reaper. Necrogeography and current ecology too.

But those are just the way that my mind works, a reflection of how I keep the balance from swinging too far out of line. The actual rituals described within these pages will work as well with classical necromancy, modern witchcraft or any number of allied esoteric disciplines. Feel free to take from this malformed mix of sometimes diametrically opposed traditions what you will, before discarding that which does not resonate.

This text is designed in a three book structure. Each of these covers one of the different roles that the adept will find themselves in during their own walk along the cemetery path. Those are further divided into chapters, and then those into individual essays. And of course I have left a little personal comment above them all, just to remind everyone of who is on the other side of the keyboard.

That is as much of me as you will see running through The Accelerated Necromancer until the afterword, though hopefully the actual content of the essays themselves will still hold my particular blend of asinine humour and iconoclastic thinking. I decided to let the ideas speak for themselves, and oh, how their voices are raised against the dreary material culture that permeates the modern world.

The first book, The Necromantic Priest, outlines much of the moral and cosmological thinking that went into the system. It also describes the many and varied seasonal observances that more chronologically minded adepts will want to try out, and offers an overview of the death current as a cultural force. It also touches upon the possible identity of the Reaper, a figure that is most definitely female in the accelerated paradigm.

The second book is The Necromantic Magus, and the title speaks for itself. An exploration of the rituals and scavenged ingredients that give this path such a distinctly earthy flavour, it also explains why you should always bring an adept on a ghost hunt. This too is where ghoulish feeding is covered, though those who were hoping for necrophagia will be sorely disappointed. Some minor healing arts are covered too.

The final book is perhaps the most grounded in material ideas. The Necromantic Hermit discuses the idea of necrogeography, or the natural accretion of death and decay in the urban environment, as well as how to harness that history. It also covers funerary rites of a kind, dispels the idea of the haunted house and jumps to the defence of the Ouija board. The blood magick and bodily decomposition essays are also here.

There is some crossover between the subjects within all the different sections, and rituals are either explicitly outlined or hinted at throughout the entire text. There is an understated line of slowly building anarchy, and by the end of the book the reader should have a good idea of how to push the boundaries of cultural taboo while also remaining mostly safe while doing so.

Ultimately The Accelerated Necromancer is designed to help the reader see the spirit world through a respectful, if at times darkly tinted, lens. There is much beauty in death, and as long as the adept does not let the balance swing too far out of line they are given a surprising amount of freedom to do as they will when using the techniques showcased here.

Acknowledgements

My humble thanks goes out to all the unsung heroes of the modern occult revival, the lone bloggers, message board denizens and social media sorcerers who left their footprints in the ever shifting sand of the digital realm for me to follow. Unverified personal gnosis is just the contents of books yet to be published, after all, and many libraries could be filled with those esoteric insights now sadly lost to time.

I also want to acknowledge the presence of the dark goddess Lilith in my life, and offer her heartfelt gratitude for pushing me to be a better sorcerer than most would have assumed a grungy and dyslexic college dropout from the poorer part of the East End of London could ever aspire to be. Hail to you, my queen of sorrows, as always I am yours.

And finally the editors at Erebus Society for taking a chance on my first solo book too. While my individual articles have seen print in numerous places over the last decade or so I am also very aware that accepting a pitch based purely on past glory and a promised deadline is far from normal in this industry. Hopefully I lived up to my part of the deal.

Dedication

This book is dedicated to the witch with the other half of my soul.

I thank the goddess that you found me, and that you love me still.

BOOK ONE

The Necromancer's Creed

Neutrality is not weakness. Long have I considered myself an explorer at the fringes of life and death, and an anarchist refusing to tow the party line when it comes to the usually dismissive or destructive attitude of the mortal realm for those who still wonder it unclothed in flesh.

Perhaps it is the more stoic aspects of my personality which find their most obvious expression through the weight which I carry as one who was called to the service of the Veil. Or maybe my nonconformist streak is highlighted against the shadows of the grave markers that I quietly show reverence while passing on by.

Regardless of the reasoning I temper much of my interaction with the unseen world through a dour sarcasm that has thus far at least kept me both safe and sane. Well, mostly anyway. We all have our scars, and when journeying into uncharted territory the only thing preventing them from reopening is a set of self imposed rules.

Balance

The necromancer is unimportant. While many see the occult as a means to test the limits of their personal will against the wider reality, this is not usually the case with the priests and priestesses of the Veil. Such blanket aggression against the flow of fate is understood as meaningless when all that they ever were will one day fade to dust.

That is not to say that approaching life's challenges with an eye to shifting the metaphorical goalposts in your favour is redundant. Magick still works, and the adept can retain personal and perhaps even social autonomy by altering their lives in line with such needs.

Yet it must be understood that these esoteric actions are not free. What fate, reality or the gods choose to give is in truth taken from somewhere else. The river of abundance does not just spring from nothing, but is instead altered in its flow to arrive in the accelerated necromancer's life instead.

There is always a price, and as the universe rushes in to fill the void created by the adept's actions it must be solemnly accepted that altering the weave on the loom may lead to a few loose ends which need to be tidied up elsewhere. It is rare to see that rebalancing occur first hand, of course, but out of sight should not mean out of mind.

The job gained through prayer to whichever deity of choice was originally fated to another, who now has none. The relationship eased into place through sigils and expertly dressed candles has left someone, somewhere alone and unloved. The spirit who was rebuffed from entering a home by that crown of thorns has gone to bother the less skilled instead.

There is no an it harm none, just a race to the top with an eye on those left behind to make sure they are not catching up. Regardless of the seemingly altruistic paradigm that many witches or sorcerers adopt, someone is destined to lose the very thing others gained through all that dedicated ritual work.

Those who dabble in the occult as a practical tool to realise their will are just thieves, and the necromancer accepts that fact as part of who they are more easily than most. This, then, is the curse of understanding, something which weighs heavily on the minds of the very few who choose to walk along the cemetery path for any length of time.

As an occult discipline which accepts that at the basic level even the continued functioning of the mortal shell requires the regular sacrifice of other living things, it is an easy enough mental leap to expand that bleak line of thought towards externalised processes such as the wider effects of spells or outcomes of prayer to the gods.

As such the adept should strive to remain proportional in their response to the events in their life, resolving what they can through mundane means and falling back on ritual only when either all other avenues are exhausted or the desired result is so bizarre in nature that it is unlikely to occur without a miracle.

This is not to say that magick should just be explored in times of crisis of course. Life as a priest or priestess of the Veil still involves regular interactions with the unseen world. Ancestors, wondering spirits, and even deity if desired are all a constant in the adept's increasingly strange life.

But when there is a chance that the actions which they take will alter the balance in such a way that it may deprive someone else of that was originally going to be theirs then that burden must be shouldered and acknowledged so as to keep the necromancer's feet planted firmly on the right cemetery path.

Heaven, Hell, Valhalla, Niflheim, Elysium, Summerland, or reincarnation. Such grand concepts are of little interest to the truly accelerated adept. Those are best dealt with when the time comes and not seen as either a threat or reward looming over life while it is being lived.

Morals are an intensely personal thing, after all, and should not be held hostage by the promise of an existence beyond the one which the person is experiencing right now. The cosmos will endure regardless of their actions, and on a large enough timescale even the most heinous of crimes is forgotten by the constant march towards modernity anyway.

As long as the necromancer can look at themselves in the mirror and accept what they see it can be assumed that their own moral compass still points in the right direction. Not everyone has the same boundaries, nor should they. But acknowledging the negative effect on others who the adept's magick pushes aside provides a far more honest way of approaching the desire for balance than that loosely defined an it harm none.

The Seven Necromantic Laws

What follows are the seven core laws that I personally live by, as compiled from my own experience. They have not been created arbitrarily, and reflect the scaffolding which kept me safe during an all too strange walk along my own cemetery path.

Yes, these rules may appear overly cautious at first, but are designed to head off many of the stumbling blocks that can cause long term health or legal issues for the more reckless adept. You are free to discard these as necessary, of course, though most definitely at your own risk.

Accelerated Necromancy may at first seem to be an unduly restrictive system for those who seek to communicate, or even exploit, the dead. With a polarity that is skewed firmly towards mutual respect, albeit while holding enough back in reserve to make any who cross the adept regret their actions, it is a discipline that promotes peace and personal reflection above all else.

When cornered on their prevailing beliefs, most priests and priestesses of the Veil will stay mute and refuse to answer, for that is not the business of the uninitiated. Knowledge is power, and to share the personal code by which they travel the cemetery path is to give others the tools to manipulate them if so desired. Best to smile knowingly and change the subject.

That said, the following more universal rules are kept in place to prevent even the most inexperienced adept from making potentially grave mistakes while exploring the unseen realms. These are what sets accelerated necromancy apart from the classical discipline which shares its name. Of course they can be broken as necessary, though it is highly ill advised to do so.

One: Respect The Journey Of The Dying

Everything ends. This is a journey usually undertaken alone, forgotten and unwanted. Pain is silenced by drugs and the inevitable decay of the physical form is hidden behind locked hospital doors. It is in the recognition of this that the necromancer comes into their own.

Sitting vigil over dying family members provides a solemn lesson in the nature of mortality, though for those who have been lucky enough to avoid such an event thus far a basic understanding of anatomy and a keen interest in autopsy will suffice. The most important thing to realise is that such remains are just meat and gristle, and of no use to the genuine adept.

Two: Respect The Remains Of The Dead

The true necromancer does not need to desecrate human remains. No bones must be burned or flesh consumed for a connection with those who have already passed to be made. Indeed, the physical aspects of the path are the preserve of those who lack the fine tuned instincts which allow for a purer relationship with the death current itself.

Shading into the psychic arts, a recognition and control of energy in all its forms is the only real prerequisite required. While there are many factors which lead someone to seek the Veil, an enduring respect for the sanctity of death is by far the most important.

Three: Respect The Places Of The Fallen

While the dead in a classical sense do not linger in graveyards, they may be called there far easier than at the necromancer's own altar. Battlefields and plague pits all hum noticeably with the death current and attract way-point seeking necrogeographic adepts like moths to a very vibrant flame.

Knowing this it makes sense to look after these already liminal spaces, and drive home the need for respect when walking there among the uniniti-ated. Vandalism to tombs and monuments should be actively discouraged if witnessed, while a local cemetery can be adopted and regularly maintained as an act of devotion as well.

Four: Respect The Spirits Of The Lost

Not all who pass arrive at their designated detonation. The necromancer may be called upon to assist in removing such stragglers from places where the living still reside, usually as a result of an incomplete upload to the Otherworld. That said, unless the pseudo-spirits are deliberately violent or threatening they should be handled with all the respect and understanding that the adept would accord their physical remains.

Dying does not wash away the negativity of the living, however, and the ghostforms of bad people generally remain so. Should the worst happen and this appear to be the case then a less polite methodology is acceptable when maintaining both the integrity of the mortal realm and the safety of its inhabitants.

Five: Respect The Scavengers At The Feast

As an unapologetically adversarial discipline, the modern necroman-cer has much to learn from the various animals that skulk in the shadows around the fringes of human habitation. Carrion feeders and vermin alike, their willingness to thrive on the items others disregard is a fitting lesson for the more creative adept.

Equally unwanted by the wider culture, those who work within the boundaries laid out through the flow of the death current must heed the wisdom of the furtive crow or cunning fox and remain hidden around those who would never understand that they are far from the grave robbing ghouls of yesteryear.

Six: Respect The Deities Of The Veil

Whichever denomination the adept adheres to, there will be one or more entities who are especially tied to the death current. Be they solemn titanic psychopomps such as Hecate or glorious warrior maidens like the Valkyries, each fulfils a much needed role within the sphere of death.

As such, the necromancer is expected to honour not only those associated with their chosen path but the numerous others who undertake the same burden for the roads not travelled. To what degree these secondary observances are made is left up to the individual, though at the very least they should be acknowledged as kindred spirits.

Seven: Respect The Guardians Of The Gate

Necromancy is undertaken by a few of those who who still breathe on behalf of the many that do not. It is a devotional path, paying heed to the importance of helping to keep the worlds of the living and the dead apart. Standing in this liminal space is no easy task, and high priests or priestesses of the death current tend to report debilitating or mysterious health issues which only grow over time.

When coupled with a loss of connection to the physical realm some become mere shells of their former selves. Far from being a negative, this draining of personal vigour is an important step that allows the adept to become a living reminder of what awaits all who will cross the Veil. There is no need to speed such a ritualistic decay of course, as it will occur naturally as the cemetery path is walked anyway.

Renting The World

I have long held a less than flattering view of my fellow man. Never a joiner I hold little faith in governments or corporations to do the right thing, nor do I see the average person willing to put the needs of the collective above their own selfish desires on a regular basis either. The tired apathy of least resistance is just too strong a force in most people's lives for them to desire change.

Yet far from finding this mistrust as alienating it instead empowers me to look beyond the here and now and treat humanity as something more than just the current crop of mortals shuffling ever closer towards an enforced journey across the Veil. As we were so those who follow us shall also be. As long as we leave them enough of a world to inherit, that is.

Necromancy has an undeserved reputation for being needlessly nihilistic. But when viewed as a path which seeks to foster harmony between the realms of the living and the dead, a far more nuanced vision of the priest or priestess of the Veil's role in the weave of fate begins to emerge.

When the idea of the adept's status as the most recent link in a chain which stretches far back into antiquity is mentioned, it is normal for those outside of the discipline to assume a commentary on the survival of some form of ancient ritual system is being described, as with the traditional witches or cabbalists who find value in such an unbroken lineage to the past.

Yet for those who stand beside the Veil the concept takes on a vastly more mundane, physical meaning. It is not an ever present sequence of adepts, nor is it the line of descendents carrying that once hidden knowledge into the far future. No, it literally just refers to family, because initiation and secrecy mean very little when there is no one left alive to inherit it.

The only thing that matters is treating the Earth with respect so others may one day walk freely upon it, living within a viable ecosystem where the sky is not bathed in fire or soil full of poison. The world does not belong to the current generation any more than it did to those who went before, and is simply being rented from those who will follow, and who follow them, and so on.

Indeed, the more open minded necromancer will often find themselves shoulder to shoulder with both ecologists and Neopagans quite regularly, even when their presence is met with scorn or mistrust. In those cases it is best to try and downplay the perceived moral shadows that many accuse them of dwelling in, and instead concentrate on the task at hand.

Reverence for the dead may not automatically create a similar interest in the sanctity of life for all who work within that paradigm, but the two do seem to go together more often than not. While the adept likely has very little free time outside of both their day to day activities and magickal experiments to spend on side projects it is not unusual for a questioning eye to be cast towards issues plaguing the wider world.

Climate change, deforestation, microplastics, the strain put on the ecosystem by fast, disposable fashion trends and the ever growing war machines of countries assuming the moral high ground down the barrel of a gun. All this and more harm the global culture of the 21st Century, and there is no indication anyone in power actually cares enough to change the script.

Piles of discarded clothing big enough to see from space and plastics small enough to make their way into the bloodstream. Rivers bursting their banks and mudslides oozing from once forested slopes above. Landmines and depleted uranium ammunition laying like terrible seeds in the soil of the poorest nations. Temperatures rising while fossil fuels choke the sunset.

Mankind is a warlike species. It is also short sighted and often fails to see the damage it is doing in the name of either progress or protection. Culture in general only ever operates on a sliding scale of a century or two either side of its current state, and it is that lack of vision which has pushed climate change to the point of no return since the industrial revolution.

Yet the access that the necromancer has to those who have lived before gives them a unique view of the flow of time itself. If any effort is dedicated to understanding how cultures grow and develop a recognition soon dawns that history as a foundation is never simply a stepping stone to get here, nor is the future guaranteed either. Both are potentially in play at any given point.

On a personal level those who care enough to try and make a change on a small scale can adopt a graveyard or similar bounded green space, picking up litter or clearing fallen branches as the chance arises. Some of those locations, especially if situated in a larger city, are designated as nature reserves though. So in general the plants and trees should be left alone no matter how overgrown.

For those with broader visions charities, unions and special interest groups can be joined in an attempt to try and wrest control of the narrative from those who care not what they do. This is best thought of as a secondary option, however, as in many cases those organisations are little better than the very corporations they seek to oppose.

In the end the adept is forced to accept that their time upon this now sadly boiling ball of mud and melting ice is but the briefest grain of sand in the Reaper's hourglass. While they have as much right to be comfortable in their surroundings as anyone else, the accelerated necromancer should act in such a way as to not disrespect the future generations who will one day be walking their own cemetery paths.

The Veiled Year

I have always been a canary in the coal mine. Indeed, my time struggling to fit in with the occasionally conservative Neopagan community has led to me becoming something of a bugbear within those groups. A grumbling, sour and sacred cow challenging voice which most would prefer not to hear no matter how valid the point.

Regardless, my conclusions about an unprecedented global blending of the death and nature currents remain valid regardless of other's opinions of me. This is a conversation which will still need to be held in the face of the distaste for my more chaotic take on the old religion, and far sooner than some may think.

That which is true does not become false just because the person shouting against the gathering storm is a divisive figure within the selfsame movements that stand to be most heavily effected by the whirling winds. Hexing the messenger is usually pointless when the facts bare out what they have to say in the end, as is sadly the case here.

Autumnal Paradigm

Gaia is wounded. The human desire to consume and innovate has caused irreversible damage to the planet, and now more than ever the entire species teeters at the edge of the abyss. But it is not a cold or dark journey to oblivion that awaits those who look away. The end of civilisation will be one of fire, not ice. Sadly, this is the brave new world that the necromancer inhabits, albeit from the sidelines.

Extreme weather events happen much more frequently now. Global temperatures are on the rise. The seas may not be boiling, but alterations to ecosystems caused by even a degree or two can be felt throughout the food chain. Everything from plankton to elephants are effected, altered and ultimately harmed by mankind's drive to take from the world without conscience.

Vocal denial of what to many appears as an onrushing apocalypse sits defiantly on the fringes of academia. Bad actors with ties to oil companies and big tech post lies and misinformation on social media and news websites alike. Populism defines policy, and the path of least cultural inconvenience wins the day. Debate becomes dogma, devolving into little more than the background hum to the twilight of humanity.

With all the chatter back and forth it can be hard for anyone to know what is true and what is fantasy. But unlike many who are faced with that wall of text and accusation, it is an uncomfortable mix of adepts who seek their spirituality through the natural world and those at the necromantic fringe who can both feel the change most strongly.

The Earth is no longer the same, and as a result the very energy that underpins the spellwork the adept attempts within that sphere has also altered. What was once a primal but calming flow of warmth has quickened, becoming less like the steady breath of an unseen matriarch and more like ragged gulps of air from overexerted lungs. Death and decay manifested in the very roots of the natural world.

While pagans and their allies try to do as little harm as possible the actions of those who care not for such considerations have collectively choked the earth goddess, and the cost of that hubris extends deep into the spiritual realm. As the planet warms and the waste piles up, so too does the nature current change. It falls to both witch and necromancer alike to recognise that shift and embrace it, or risk being left behind entirely.

There is a small but noticeable sickness underscoring the energies produced by the natural world now. An indistinct miasma can be tasted on the back of the tongue when meditating in those ever shrinking green spaces. No matter how strong the force produced by even the most remote of locations it will still be there, like an itch at the borders of the mind that refuses to go away. The death current waxes in power.

According to some the point of no return has been reached, and catastrophic climate change is now inevitable. But to be clear, this man made slide into abyss will not be quick. While the summers will be oppressively warm and the seasons shift and coalesce into one long dust bowl, it could be many years before the most dire effects of the wanton destruction of the planet will be felt.

Considering the recent claims that rainwater is no longer safe to drink anywhere on the planet due to chemical contamination, or that many of the coastal waters around more populated countries are little better than open sewers, there is more to fear from the predicted rise in sea level than just a loss of real estate.

The Earth is in conflict with a population who incorrectly believe that the entire bounty of existence is theirs for the taking. And if the essence of the nature current has shifted to something more akin to that of a dying animal rather than a dormant giant then that is how it must be approached by those who still find value in doing so.

An autumnal paradigm must emerge, one that accepts that the natural world is now changing, becoming permanently blended with the very death current which many necromancers choose to call home. There is no point in blaming the messengers, because those who seek the Veil take no pride in the cancer eating away at the green. Nor are they to blame for the damage which has been done to Gaia either.

Regardless of overarching belief all those who work with the energies inherent in nature will have already noticed that the results of their rituals seem increasingly chaotic, tinged with a melancholy that seems to be slowly growing in intensity as the broken wheel of the year turns. Over time this will lead to more failures and added difficulty in attaining predictable results.

Worse, as existing farmland dries out or is lost to the sea and nutrient rich locations to clear for agriculture become scarce there will be an inevitable slide further towards genetic modification as the only way to keep an ever exploding population clothed and fed.

While the long term benefits or otherwise of such corporate led tampering on the mundane level are up for debate there has been little talk about how such fundamental editing of a given material could forever alter its occult properties. This change will inevitably effect the majority of the plants, herbs and spices which are required for some traditional forms of witchcraft or magick.

Worse, due to the coming stagnation of the nature current many of these items may no longer be viable, and could end up removed from the food chain entirely. Of course, mankind will strive to survive the bleak world they have created. It has never been a species willing to go quietly when faced with darker times ahead, though their focus on attacking problems instead of mitigating them will likely lead to a sad end.

Forced to put further strain upon the ecosystems of this planet through panicked consumption of natural resources it will become apparent all too late that such desperate harvesting can only hasten the unwanted blending of the nature and death currents. Earth as a ball of rock spinning through space will survive. But this iteration of the green world may well be doomed to die with the people who refused to see the truth.

Yet it is needlessly pessimistic to view mankind as a parasite, or a viral strain infecting the Earth's natural order. An autumnal paradigm would not deny the human need to create, or rail against modernity. But those who feel the pull of the slowly growing sickness in the once refreshing primal energies of our planet must accept that a price for those advancements will eventually need to be paid.

And oh, how the spirits of old stir as the world becomes bathed in fire. Pazuzu threads locusts through the farmlands, spreading famine in his wake. Typhon towers over villages with indiscriminate lightning and devouring winds, pushing the people in an ever widening path to the brink of destruction.

Jealous Poseidon unleashes the tides upon the land reclaimed from the oceans by human ingenuity, taking what was once his without thought for the cost. And Helios has no choice but to turn the soil to dust as his once empowering rays become trapped within the gas choked atmosphere below.

It is too late to avert the ire of the individual gods and goddesses who were once called upon to keep those events at bay in less industrial times. Science and mythology rarely intersect, and to fall back into mysticism when dealing with the changes to the ecosystem would be a dangerous waste of time.

But a certain level of personification is healthy when metabolising such disasters, even if the cause is definitely more physical than spiritual. Humanity will, as always, bring their deities with them into the gathering twilight, though how they will be altered by that shift towards darkness remains to be seen.

In truth Gaia also stands apart from such veneration, a vast and impossibly complex hyperobject that is beyond the adept's ability to heal through prayer and assumed goodwill. While efforts to curtail the damage that individuals are responsible for on the physical plane remain worthwhile in the

14

short term, those who actually care cannot alter what has been done to the Earth through their actions alone.

And knowing how little the rest of society actually thinks about the world they live on there is nothing left to do but accept how she will change before the adept's tear filled eyes. Perhaps this shift finally signals the evolution of the earth goddess from nurturing Mother to harsh Crone on some fundamental yet mystical level, paving the way for a twilight of the goddess.

Considering the age, wisdom and tacit acceptance of death encapsulated in that latter archetype, it seems fitting for the autumnal paradigm that seems to be slowly waxing within esoteric thought. It would also suit the reducing bounty of the soil as ecosystems collapse and mass extinctions take hold. There is always a price when the balance is ignored, and too few are willing to pay to reset that pendulum swing.

Unfortunately, whether this revelation resonates with those outside of the necromantic paradigm or clashes with their worldview has become irrelevant. To impishly paraphrase Fyodor Dostoevsky completely out of context, nature does not ask permission. It could care less about whether people choose to agree with or refute what it seems to say.

As the overarching operating system that all life on Earth relies upon it retains the balance of power in such negotiations, even in an increasingly weakened state. Because change is now inevitable. As mankind takes more the nature current will have no choice but to offer less.

While a concerted effort by Earth's entire population could slow this progress towards the collective Veil, the damage that has already been done up to this point will cripple Gaia even as she tries to heal. And as the most perceptive of her children with regards to the waxing death current, the necromantic community must now bear the weight of that diseased autumnal wind more than most.

The Broken Wheel

It was sadly inevitable that the more classically pagan practices which I observed would become tinged with a miasma of rot and decay as the autumnal paradigm took hold. This then is the result. My revised wheel of the year, a personal attempt to describe the changes going on around me as the death current waxes and wanes in time with the shifting seasons.

It is missing the spokes intended for Imbolc and Lammas, as they fail to resonate with either my necromantic lifestyle or the cyclic journey of Persephone. Beltane is observed as Walpurgisnacht instead to better metabolise the energies of Samhain at its opposite point in the cycle, while also paying homage to witches of yesteryear. It is all just Folklore of course, though like many myths has a far deeper meaning.

Mabon

The start of the necromantic wheel of the year and the beginning of Persephone's journey to the underworld, the autumn equinox is also the time where her mother, Demeter, retreats from her godly duties and sits in sorrow, waiting until her beloved daughter returns in the spring. As a goddess directly tied to both corn and the harvest, it is her refusal to offer the world of man year long bounty that causes the cycle of the seasons.

Allegory perhaps, but borne out in the changes occurring in the nature current around this time. Nights are lengthening and, despite the ever warming world, should be all the cooler too. In rural landscapes harvests have now been brought in, larders stocked with grain and preserved meats. Fruit becomes harder to come by and hearty stews are back on the menu along with root vegetables and flaming spices.

The urban adept is likely to miss much of this interplay between the still ascendant nature current and the slowly waxing death current, though it can still be felt in their bones. As with much in the built landscape it is man made calenders as opposed to natural instincts which show time passing, though the graveyards that they claimed during the warmer months will likely be resplendent in their autumn glory.

The necromancer cannot help but marvel at the way the colours shift through the leaves. Red, gold. Dirty brown, all that once was lush and green begins to wane as summer is overpainted by a pallet of rusty hues. Conkers and chestnuts fall like treasures from the tired trees. Mosses and mushrooms take root. Small mammals look for a bolthole to weather the upcoming winter storms.

As it was with the people of old, this is a perfect time to take stock, weigh up magick done and sorcery yet to be completed. Desired changes to the adepts life can be taken below the soil with Persephone using rituals designed to incubate those much needed boons within the womb of the earth. These will then grow in the spring along with her return.

This is also a great time for the necromancer to walk their home city, dodging the showers as they witness the frost and fog begin to form on otherwise sun choked streets. Offering bowls overflow with dried herbs and fallen nuts, though care should be exercised if candles are to be burned at their centre due to how easily these can catch fire.

All in all the adept should metabolise as much of the decay and slowly draining vitality as possible, drawing it into themselves and learning to turn that blended current over in their minds eye. It will be needed for what lies ahead, for the biggest annual test of the Veil's integrity is but a month away.

Samhain

As the Veil shuts its invisible gates around Persephone and torch bearing Hekate ushers the goddess below to judge those lost souls which fall under her sway, so too does the fabric of reality groan under the collective weight of all those who came before. This is because Samhain, as well as a few days either side, is by far the easiest time to break bread with the dead.

Yes, different cultures set aside other dates to recognise their spirits. But Halloween rides across the English speaking world like the wild hunt itself, hell hounds baying for the blood of the damned while children dress as comic book characters and seek out technicolour chocolate offerings door to door.

The nights are both longer and colder now. The dark creeps in through uncurtained windows, pooling in the corners of the room and resisting the light as it settles in for the harsh winter to come. Homes whisper and creak, an audible flexing of the Veil as their history begins to repeat itself in front of a captive audience.

This is the busiest time of the year for those who walk the cemetery path. Indeed the necromancer will feel a two pronged swelling of the death current around this four or so week period, as not only is there a definite upswing in paranormal activity as October comes to a close but also unironic public interest in topics usually reserved for the adept alone.

This window of enhanced opportunity is finite, however, and drops off sharply a few days after Halloween, taking the more informational groundswell within the death current with it too. The more energetic aspects will retain their ascendency until late November though. The adept should concentrate on ancestor work around this time, as well as operations designed to amplify the necromantic aspects of their other magicks

Dumb suppers can be arranged, completely silent meals that include favourite foods of the deceased. A more filling variation on the classic séance, these sombre but tasty events can help even the most psychically challenged of people feel the influence of the death current in their lives. A more general menu would boast classically necromantic items such as rare steak and burnt bread.

Graveyards can be reclaimed for another year, though it is ill advised to do this on Halloween itself due to the heightened security around burial plots at that observance. Wards and bindings can also be renewed, defences against either wandering spirits or ghostforms put in place to help the adept keep themselves and their families safe until the broken wheel turns again.

Yule

The cold and barren manifestation of Persephone's underworld imprisonment, the time around Yule is a sign of things to come should the natural world be forced to struggle to survive in the wake of mankind's ever grasping hands. The death current is in full control during those longest nights, claiming the old and infirm far more easily than in the height of summer.

While the minds of the uninitiated masses in the northern hemisphere may be blinded by Christmas, itself little better than a gallows feast to keep mortal spirits high in the face of winter's ever icy grip, the necromancer sees those joyous religious distractions for exactly what they really are.

This period may be bleak, but also grants a useful reminder to even the most oblivious adept that despite all the modern comforts of hearth and home an absence of natural growth in any closed system is to be feared instead of celebrated. And in a potentially barren universe that seems to actively resist exploration through sheer hostility, the ecology of the Earth is more closed than most.

The necromancer will retreat into themselves around this time. They willingly take on board a similar forced hibernation as the trees which now claw sadly against the ashen sky. Storms are likely, and snow too. A general prayer can be intoned to the unknown dead who lost their lives while struggling against the bad weather, their remains only discovered after the spring thaw.

This ever tightening cold creeps into the bones and can, in moderation, be used to help the adept work with the numbness that awaits them as they near the end of their journey towards the Veil. Warm clothing should be on hand when conducting such operations outside, just in case, and laying in the cold for any more than five minutes or so without such preparation is not recommended.

Icicles and snow can be harvested from tombs and grave markers to be used as a liquid base for ritual washes and candle dressings, though should not be consumed in any form due to the pollution now sadly circulating within the water table worldwide.

Wreaths of holly and mistletoe are a great way to bring evergreen energy into an otherwise solemn observance, a much needed reminder that while the land has fallen under the sway of the biting wind the nature current is not completely beaten. At least not yet.

Ostara

The spring equinox brings promises of hope as Persephone travels from the underworld to the lands of men, bringing her mother's natural energies back to the thankfully warming earth. A time of newly made plans as the wheel of the year turns towards the warmer months ahead, it is not unusual to see even the most sour of necromancers open up a little around this time.

While the uninitiated play at painting eggs and drown in cheaply produced chocolate treats, the adept will likely ignore Easter unless family pull them into those highly caloric celebrations. Their attention is instead upon observing the sluggishly waxing life force which is now pushing up from beneath the soil, as well as enjoying the many rainy days which will help that green world grow.

Wildlife returns to gardens and open spaces, while grasses begin to gather around the wildflowers which are giving the graveyard a much needed burst of colour. And all the while, birds are nesting, awaiting the many chicks that will be born in the months ahead. The promise of summer is ever present as the days start to lengthen.

Necromancy is the study of life force in all its forms. While Easter is of little importance to the adept, honouring as it does the assumed resurrection of a figure who has had untold atrocities done in their name, the rising nature current should be at least acknowledged as the balance swings away from the dead as central figures in the seasonal narrative.

They should not fear this forced movement into a more Neopagan space, and indeed the willingness to engage with the greener aspects of the budding landscape are a welcome shift in perspective after the long nights spent in mental isolation around Yule. As such it is a perfect time to wander beyond the ritual chamber and observe this natural incursion within otherwise urban sprawls.

Showers are in full swing, and storm water collected during this waxing of the nature current has a unique charge to it which is absent after spring ages towards summer. It is an effervescent overabundance, a churning expression of growth energy given fluid form. Worth grabbing for healing washes if nothing else, though again definitely not safe to drink.

A ritualised planting of flower seeds in a walled garden or window box can be undertaken to grant the necromancer a microcosmic view of the birth, growth, death cycle, and herbs can be set side by side with these to add a little freshness to future ritual blends. For those uncomfortable with such naked abundance, a little grave dirt can be mixed into the soil to calm it down.

Walpurgisnacht

A worthy counterpoint to Samhain on the necromancer's broken wheel of the year, the usually fiery Beltane energy is instead inverted and replaced with stridently feminine lunar essence as Persephone and Demeter hold court upon the very tip of the Brocken. Surrounded by all the witches who journey to be with them they dance around the need fires on the mountain top, nature and death currents both swirling in their wake.

Tales of such Walpurgisnacht sabbaths have long troubled the minds of the uninitiated in Europe, while the Bavarian Hexennacht is celebrated with costumes and revelry in a similar vein to Halloween. Just a local observance, of course, but one that carries a far greater weight for the adept who is willing to rehabilitate the very same folklore which once consigned heretics to the pyre.

Longer spring evenings begin to inject memories of summers past into the orange tinged dusk. Foxes yip in the night, their eyes balls of burning Beltane fire as they slink between the bins and alleyways that criss-cross the urban sprawl. Owls hoot overhead as they hunt for prey. Crows and rooks scavenge in gardens. Insects land on damp grass as it sways long and green against the first rays of dawn.

The adept would do well to respect these energies of abundance. Remember, even in her wounded state Gaia remains far more powerful than the most belligerent priest or priestess of the Veil will ever be. And due to accelerated necromancy being a celebration of life force in all its forms as opposed to just decay alone, there is no reason why those warmer nights cannot be enjoyed anyway. Balance is key, after all.

Now is a good time to blow sweet smelling incenses through the home, as well undertaking a general tidying of the magical workspace. This will also work as an energetic cleansing too, trapping and carrying away negative emotions while the spring breeze mingles with the swirling wisps of charcoal, amber resin and lavender that pop and hiss on the altar.

Graveyards begin to open later after the dark winter months, and both these and the wider corpse ways are far easier to map as a result. Grave dirt may be difficult to harvest around this time due to the persistent showers, though the abundance of moisture and the warmer weather does bode well for those who are looking to take a few wild garlic leaves back home with them.

Walpurgisnacht and the surrounding weeks are a perfect time for exploration within the adept's built landscape. The entire city should now be a viable ritual space, as any necrogeographic work the accelerated necromancer is looking to do is better undertaken in late spring as opposed to the overly oppressive midsummer heat.

Litha

As the solstice burns away the clouds overhead Persephone continues the ever slowing spring dance in the sunlight of the longest day, a wildflower in her hair. Yet even this summer reverie is tinged with sadness at the journey she will soon be forced to undertake, slave as she is to the whims and desires of other gods.

Demeter has gone back to oversee the growth of the crops that will be harvested later in the calender year, and the witches have returned to their homes after the excesses of the Brocken. This is a lonely time of expectations and sorrow for Persephone, as the warmth of the earth also signals an inevitable return to the cold of the grave for her all too soon.

Tarot and rune readings for the next turn of the broken wheel are best undertaken around this time, and questions asked of deities before the death current begins to wax in power during the underworld portion of Persephone's cyclic journey. Do not forget that the darker half of the year starts as soon as the solstice itself ends, albeit slowly at first, and certain godesses are unwilling to grant boons during those months.

Necromantic operations of clearing and banishing will be especially effective on Litha itself, as the solar energy can be called to flood the target location and overwrite the rogue echoes or shards that call such places home. This is also a rare occasion where the adept may perform such an operation during the daylight hours as opposed to after nightfall and still expect success.

For those who are lucky enough to have garden spaces attached to their home this is a perfect opportunity to turn such yard work into a ritualistic act of green husbandry as preparations for the rise of autumn and eventually winter are made. As always, those without such a connection to the nature current can visit and tidy their adopted graveyard instead.

The necromancer would do well to look upon Persephone's sadness at the assumed abundance of this season as allegory for the end which awaits their mortal frame as well. They should need no excuse to enjoy the pleasures of the flesh, albeit responsibly, before it is lost to the soil. There is a reason why the broken wheel ends in the hot summer months, as it shows even the most stubborn adept that change is a constant.

This recognition is not a call to hedonism but an appeal to honesty instead. Because in a universe where the Otherworld is not guaranteed there is no sense in wasting the only life one may ever get pretending to be someone else to make others happy. As such, Litha is a time of endings, even if this flies in the face of the overarching themes of what is usually understood to be a fiery and positive observance.

Calender Applications

Of course I rarely pass up the chance to take part in some form of ritual, especially when there is an ever evolving narrative adding some underlying purpose to the proceedings. And while the broken wheel is a great way to actively engage with the cycles of the seasons through the tale of Persephone and Demeter, there are ways to do the same with the actual dead, too.

These monthly new moon observances are a simple yet effective way to show reverence for those who crossed the Veil through sometimes harrowing circumstances, and I use them to remind me that not everything in my life as as dire as it at first appears. It also adds a reassuring regularity to the background hum of my altar space, as well as leaving some intriguingly cryptic lingering energies too.

While the broken wheel lays out the general structure of the accelerated necromancer's year, the monthly observances which occur alongside those more notable semi-seasonal celebrations are equally important. Indeed the ritual framework adopted by the priest or priestess of the Veil will take advantage of as many new moon rituals as the year has to offer, either twelve or thirteen depending on the way the dates fall.

The inherent ties that the darkness above has to the lightless caverns of the underworld below makes those sightless nights a perfect time to connect with the death current in a more meaningful way. And how this is done is surprisingly simple, requiring very little preparation outside of a few easily obtainable herbs or food items, a coloured candle, and a safe place to let it burn for a few hours.

Because of geographic location, daylight savings or other alterations to the flow of recorded time these pitch black rites need not be undertaken at the exact second that the moon becomes completely invisible. As with those conducted by other traditions who instead mark the fullness of the lunar disk, the closest nightfall either side is fine.

One: Serf's Moon

Generally tied to the harvest moon, September's necromantic new moon observance is dedicated to those who lost their lives in farming accidents throughout the ages. Even before the adoption of heavy machinery the dangers posed by impact wounds were made all the worse by a lack of reliable methods for treating internal injuries. Their passing is honoured with a brown candle rolled in oats.

Two: Ancestor's Moon

October, holding as it does Halloween and the blood moon is a time to recognise the spirits of the adept's own ancestors, both near and far. The new moon ritual calls upon those departed souls for wisdom, strength, and the serenity to accept that one day all that the necromancer has built will return to dust. A black candle is burned, and dressed with a few drops of blood freely given by all those in attendance.

Three: Butcher's moon

November's dark full moon would once have signalled an end to the culling of animals that were unlikely to make it through the winter, and the active preserving of their meat. Here the adept takes a moment during the new moon to think about those who, through war or disaster, were unable to be buried as a complete body in full. A red candle rolled in allspice is a suitable offering to honour those unfortunate people.

Four: Traveller's Moon

The long nights full moon of December is usually associated with celebration. Yet this was once a dangerous time to be abroad in the driving snow or bitter cold, and many a poor traveller lost their lives walking in circles while the air froze in their lungs. This new moon observance is undertaken to offer those lost souls some recognition, and a bright blue candle rolled in ground coffee works just fine to do so.

Five: Miner's Moon

Associated with the cold full moon, the subterranean workings of many tin, coal and silver mines would have offered a welcome respite from the biting January chill. Yet the drier air and slippery conditions added to the already dangerous task of taking much needed minerals from within the Earth. The new moon ritual designed to honour those who died underground involves a dark copper candle dressed with liquorice.

Six: Fisherman's Moon

Winter was a dangerous time to be away from land, and considering that many sailors could not swim getting caught in a storm around February's quickening full moon could very easily lead to a watery grave. Yet the coastal villages had to be fed as food stores from the previous year began to run low. This new moon observance recognises the courage of those lost to the waves with a turquoise candle rolled in sea salt.

Seven: Foundling's Moon

Early March has long been the lambing season in rural cultures, and the storm full moon is usually seen as a sign that the birthing cycle has peaked. The adept chooses to transmute this time of abundance into one that offers solace for those orphaned children who died young and unwanted instead. A pink or candy-striped candle generously dressed with brown sugar is offered to honour those tragic souls at the new moon.

Eight: Militia's Moon

April sees both the growing full moon and a noticeable upturn in the weather. Historically this was deemed the perfect time to mobilise the peasantry for prolonged military campaigns and while there are many monuments to professional soldiers those unnamed and unskilled masses also deserve to be remembered as well. A pale green candle rolled in garlic and burned on the new moon is a valid way to do so.

Nine: Martyr's Moon

With Walpurgisnacht over and the embers of the Beltane fires still warm, the time around May's flower full moon is usually a celebration of the new life to come. Yet the necromancer chooses instead to honour those who were hung, burned or drowned for the spurious crime of witchcraft, and the new moon ritual focusses on remembering those usually non-Pagan martyrs by burning a gold candle dressed with chilli flakes.

Ten: Companion's Moon

The honey full moon of June is usually associated with carnal passions inflamed by the longest day of the year, yet the Adept chooses this new moon to recognise the many female victims of violence who were unjustly taken from the world. And yes, this is a good time to weave protection spells around the living for similar reasons too. A white candle rolled in dried apple is used to show those souls all due respect.

Eleven: Scholar's Moon

July holds the blessing full moon and as any necromancer will recognise, knowledge is the greatest boon of all. That said adepts of many paths die before their esoteric insights are widely shared, their genius unrecognised and occulture left unaware of the leaps and bounds that they made while studying in private. Those unknown trailblazers are honoured by burning a purple candle dressed with sage on the new moon.

Twelve: Crofter's Moon

As the name would suggest, August's corn full moon is a time of harvest, busy days and abundance. Yet food security is only a constant should Gaia decide to offer up her bounty, and as a result many have died from failed crops and drought choked fields. The new moon ritual undertaken during those late summer nights offers solace to those who crossed the Veil hungry, and an orange candle rolled in sunflower seeds is burned.

Thirteen: Reaper's Moon

A black of thirteenth new moon can occur at any point during the year, and when it does it shares the month with another. While the adept may choose to double down on the ritual for that period, essentially performing it twice in a row, they can also use this time to make offerings to the Reaper herself. If this is chosen then a silver candle is burned on the extra new moon, dressed in the tears of all those in attendance.

The Holistic Adept

Necromancers such as myself tend to have a reputation for sour misanthropy, at least among the select few who know that our hearts lie with such forbidden things. To be fair, this is warranted in most cases, though no adept who truly sought to uphold the balance would seek to live exclusively within the part of the swing that occurs in the shadows.

There are just too many interesting things going on out in the weirder world for that to be a worthwhile focus. I have had my fair share of friendships, relationships and family drama over the years. There is no point in running from the life knocking at your chamber door, as without a full experience of what it means to be a mortal being it would be impossible to understand those that no longer are.

But a certain grimness of character is normal I suppose. We are the priests and priestesses of the Veil after all. The truth of that responsibility rests heavily on our shoulders as the broken wheel turns from year to year. Still, this lifestyle is a choice. Few are outright forced to walk among the endless ranks of gravestones looking for answers. What I do is done because it is important, and that at least makes me smile.

Embracing Life

More so than earthy witch or heavenly sorcerer it is mindset which truly sets the accelerated necromancer apart from others who look for answers in the dark. The mechanics of spell and ritual aside, how those potentially damned spiritual explorers stand to face another day is what makes them who they are.

Many outsiders to the art watch those upon the cemetery path with a mix of confusion and disgust. The dead sleep soundly, they say. The spirits of the ancestors only come back to help the living in times of need. The Otherworld, Heaven, Hell, those are immutable concepts. To fixate upon the afterlife while still drawing breath is a waste of time.

Nothing could be further from the truth. A healthy respect for the Veil as a barrier that permeates every inch of the material plane and understanding of the final journey which all are eventually destined to make across it can only bring solace to those that willingly accept the weight. Opening up to that inevitability is the first step to accepting the transience of all things. This too shall pass, and not always quietly.

It does not help that necromancy tends to get a raw deal in popular culture. Indeed, characters associated with this most misunderstood paradigm fall into two distinct camps. The horror film villain with an army of the resurrected dead and almost eternal lifespan, or the unlikely hero who utilises the fallen in a last ditch effort to do evil for the greater good.

The modern adept is actually far more concerned with life force in all its myriad forms than either of these fantasy stereotypes. Especially skilled practitioners will instinctively recognise the energy inherent in bodily fluids, bioelectric fields and even the everyday environment, bending a fragment of it to their will.

Coupled with years of esoteric study this understanding allows them to manipulate said flow of power to either heal or harm as desired, albeit by very small amounts at a time. It is not an easy process, nor is it guaranteed to generate results. But when it does work it works miracles, and sometimes that is exactly what they need to keep going.

Those toiling within a more classical necromantic paradigm may seek exclusively to compel spirits to appear at their behest as did the infamous historical sorcerers of old. Lusting after either treasure or wisdom, those egoistic sorcerers pester the discarnate with questions and demands, rarely getting the vastly unimportant answers that they seek from those who dream beyond the Veil.

It is a dangerous misconception that the dead are any more honest or wise than the living, one that stems from incorrect religious ideas about the nature of the afterlife. Despite new age claims otherwise a good portion of the recently deceased do not become undergrads at some infinitely vast cosmic university while they await a new posting within the material plane.

Many never completely cross to the afterlife, remaining here in a state of confusion instead. These ghostforms and echoes are the majority of the entities that the priest or priestess of the Veil will encounter on a daily basis. In light of this, a few more socially minded adepts might prefer to dwell where the forbidden arts shade into modern mediumship, serving as a tool for reunion between the living and the lost.

The caustic influence of spiritualism, with its dual vices of heretical Christianity and blatant falsification of evidence, has done much to damage this branch of the esoteric family tree. Still, there is nothing inherently wrong with training to become a clairvoyant or similar if approached honestly.

Yet anyone with a truly balanced viewpoint should realise that to narrow their interests in such a way is to also drain much of the positivity from an already unfairly maligned paradigm. And those who push on past this point will inevitably become so attuned to the ebb and flow of life force that they can instinctively recognise its ever ticking drumbeat running through all living things.

The suitably skilled necromancer easily notices when the tempo is speeding up or slowing down, and can make educated guesses as to when someone is about to make their final journey beyond the Veil. Such a power can become a burden, however, especially as it only provides insight into the basic health of the target and cannot be used to predict random or accidental deaths. It remains a grim responsibility in any case.

With dedicated practice an adept may even become powerful enough to alter the Reaper in her path, though this can only ever be done at a heavy price and never for more than a few days at most. The balance can be swung only so far in one direction before it returns to right itself. Truths always out in the end.

Death is a force much more powerful than even the most advanced student of the necromantic arts. Its darkly cowled avatar can rarely be bargained with and will not be denied forever. Sadly, this is not a path to immortality, and even the best among the priests and priestesses of the Veil will never become a kingly lich or lowly revenant. Only medical science can grant such boons.

As such it is no surprise that accelerated necromancers strongly support the case for singularity, the inevitable blending of man and machine that has

31

become a staple of science fiction. Unfortunately, this advance is staunchly opposed by the blinkered religious majority who see the idea of improving upon the human form as somehow Satanic.

But those damned few who are willing to push the limits of what is socially acceptable understand that all magick is an invasive and violent discipline wherein every advance in knowledge must be paid for through blood and toil. When such a cemetery path has already been chosen the logical next step was always going to be altering the body through science. Any means necessary to live to fight another day.

Yes, the necromancer has a reputation in popular culture for being a dark character willing to do whatever it takes to extend their already unnaturally long lives. Unethical experiments, bloodletting, the torture and draining of others to retain as much as they can of their mortal shell long past its sell by date. Fiction states as much, and while those tools are available in the real world they do not work how the majority think.

Though a heart of ice can aid the adept in weathering the storm of pleading spirits and painful personal losses it is not mandatory. There is no rule that states emotional connections are forbidden, not should there be. Lives well lived bring joy to the Reaper when she comes to claim them, after all.

All things will end. This includes those loved and hated, good deeds and bad are both forgotten should enough time pass. Cultures rise and fall, millions upon millions of stories told and retold and then rendered silent by the weight of years. On a geological scale entire countries are no more than specks of dust in the wind, even less when cosmic time shows the Earth itself to be inconsequential alongside its peers.

Nothing really matters except that which the adept chooses to invest with such personal meaning. This should not be seen as a rallying call to live as an ascetic outside of material concerns, of course. Bills must be paid, relationships fostered, a balance between the living and the dead who flow like competing corpse choked rivers through the necromancer's life maintained.

In the end there is no single initiation into service of the Veil. No grand ritual nor sacred rites associated with taking the mantle of priest or priestess of those solemn mysteries. But those very same personal connections which the fictional necromancer usually avoids are in truth the key to understanding how that unseen world should be approached.

The death of a loved one, mass slaughter witnessed or sickness eating silently away at those who the adept truly cares about. The failure of the mortal shell, arthritis deforming joints and greying hair. A quick and bloody passing or slow descent into old age. Bleary eyes opening for yet another day as the body resists the urge to move. Gravity crushing paper thin skin into the bones beneath. Quiet release.

These, then, are the initiatory lessons of the Veil, each a bittersweet tale of prior connection and fleeting flesh. And as the ticking slows and the life force ebbs from those the necromancer has built their world around, therein will they find their true calling. Loss is inevitable, but never the entire story. To feel that pain is to remember the pleasures of yesteryear, after all.

And it must be understood that this art is not one of sorrow. The burden of acceptance is in truth a boon, for once the inevitable end to the adept's mortal frame is welcomed then nothing but wide eyed adventure can wait for them as they walk across the Veil. Balance is the nature of things, after all, and without the prospect of death the experience of life would itself be meaningless.

The Honour System

While I acknowledge the balance as a core principle of the accelerated necromancer's creed, the inevitable next question is always how that is put into practice where the dead are concerned. A fair line of inquiry, and a fundamental cornerstone of the art. For once, the answer is relatively simple too, though does involve wading through a few grey areas to get there.

There is some variation as all adepts will approach this part of the paradigm a little differently, tuned as it is towards their own background and moral compass. So my live and let live attitude, even towards those who no longer do, is likely to be far mellower than the more aggressive pro mortality stance held by younger adepts. I should know, as that was my viewpoint for many years too.

One of the defining features which sets accelerated necromancy apart from the more classical version is the way that practitioners swear to a blanket respect for the remains of the dead. No summoning circles of salt next to ripped open graves, trails of rose petals or iron stakes when the conversation is over. Desecration is anathema to the genuine priest or priestess of the Veil.

This also extends to the spirits that are encountered upon the corpse ways of the urban sprawl. Whether they believe that those unseen haunts are left over information coalesced into a thoughtform of sorts, or a literal expression of a once mortal being's now immortal soul, the attitude of quiet restraint remains unchanged.

That said there is also something approaching an honour system in place. Not everything that goes bump in the night is friendly, nor do bad people automatically get absolved of their flaws once their flesh decays. As an energetic expression of who they were in life, the dead are just as capable of violence and hate as their still living counterparts. They are just harder to hold to account for their actions, is all.

The adept is not bound to a set of commandants which force them to turn the other cheek when crossed, and a proportional response is allowed when dealing with both the living and the discarnate. Actions have consequences, however. So if that retaliation, no matter how justified, would result in further personal harm then it is perhaps better to put the coffin nails and wax effigies away to move on to better things.

A warning in in order here. Allies tend to be few upon this journey to the Veil, and the less than respectable company that many necromancer's keep is a direct result of a grim acceptance by those at the fringes of counterculture. And when isolated in such a way it is only natural for the seeker to fall back on spirit communication for solace, and find companionship in the whispering walls.

This is a very dangerous state of mind. The adept should never blindly trust what is said by spirits when being encountered through Ouija boards or in séance rooms. This extends to divinatory practices involving the Veil in general. A figurative pinch of salt will do more than just keep negative entities at bay in this case, and allow for a reasoned evaluation of the results gained through those oblique communications.

In truth the priest or priestess of the Veil sees little distinction between the living and the dead, though will usually gravitate towards the rights of the physical over the spiritual in matters of territory or conflict here on the material plane. Home team rules, as they say.

It is not unusual for the necromancer's unique set of skills to be requested when a home needs clearing and suspected ghosts are to be sent somewhere else. This is not a call to arms that must be heeded, however. The adept should work to an inherent hierarchy of needs for their safety, starting with the personal, then the criminal, before they even think about tackling the supernatural.

And if the request feels wrong, seems to have more to do with a fractured mortal mind than a spiritual threat, then perhaps the safest answer is to just politely decline. While Scooby-Doo was wrong, and the monsters are not always human, there are still plenty out there who are. At least for now, until the Reaper catches up with them of course.

Over time working relationships with certain groups of spirits may begin to develop. This is either a result of familial ties, as with revered ancestors, or a continued flow of good information. Thus an honour system of sorts remains in place, one which grades these unseen helpers on results and not words. Of all the entities encountered by the adept as they walk their cemetery path, few will prove to be worth keeping around.

Yes, they are mercenaries all, and paid through the necromancer's attention and perhaps even life force for their services. Because even the dead need to eat, even if the only real food they can utilise to sustain their existence is the very same conversation which allows them to stay relevant, and therefore remain whole.

Indeed that is the secret mechanism that holds both the wondering dead and those who have crossed to the Otherworld together after their bodies have returned to the soil. Because any prolonged association between living people with mediumistic abilities and that latter group stored on the other side of the Veil will gift such distant voices the energy to continue to learn and evolve.

This is an unavoidable side effect of the living spending time around the dead, interfering as it does with the once final state of the personality as it originally crossed over. It makes them subject to the action of time yet again, for as long as the conversation occurs, and can cause distress for everyone involved if done without proper planning.

Hastily scrawled summoning circles in church crypts are a universally bad idea. Not only do they betray a predisposition towards shoddy workmanship, but if the adept is suitably skilled then they are redundant anyway. Here the honour system reflects back on the necromancer and charges them with the geas that they must give respect to expect that in return from the unseen world.

Should those once trusted spirits seem to betray the necromancer, perhaps by regularly gifting useless information through Ouija or hiding items within the living space, then ties should be cut and banishing performed as needed. There are plenty more ghosts in the aether, so there is little reason to continue with a toxic friendship by virtue of convenience. As an aside, the same can be said for gods and goddesses too.

While the alarmist or overtly religious will of course cry foul of the idea of trafficking with the dead, there is no real risk to the adept unless those conversations become more important than real world interactions. If the séance table is used as a crutch to help the wounded priest or priestess of the Veil calm their unsteady nerve then the danger of obsession becomes all too real.

So it would do the necromancer well to remember that spirits in general, regardless of whether they are seen as externalised thought forms or the true lost souls of the deceased, gain something from each interaction that is undertaken in their presence. They want to think, to feel. And the living are the only potential meal on the menu which can provide the necessary bioelectric nutrients to do so.

Upon This Cemetery Path

When I was younger I had no issues peering into the spirit world. Fearing those who dwelled within it I suppressed what I could and then accidentally burnt out what remained as swirling nightmares held my early teen years in their icy grip. This all left me as psychic as a house brick, and as I grew the realisation of what I had in fact lost haunted me more than the ghosts ever did.

So I set out to retrain myself from the few sources available at the time, using chaos magick techniques to piece together a uniquely utilitarian necromancy as I fought to recapture the spirit of those early days. But then that is just my story. Everyone who is called to the Veil will have a unique origin all their own. One undeniable truth unites us all though. What we do is done for the good of our tribe.

Ritual, no matter how complex the steps or miraculous the predicted outcome, is useless without a definite purpose. And while the accelerated necromancer must ultimately choose very personal goals while walking along the cemetery path, there is an overarching narrative that they are destined to become a part of simply by virtue of their presence among the tombstones.

Deciding to live as a priest or priestess of the Veil is exactly what it sounds like, a position of reverent custody wherein the adept shoulders the burden of Persephone's journey into the underworld to bring liminal insights back to their people. It is more of a calling than a skill set, a deep rooted need than a hobby. Despite claims of free will life tends to lead the chosen few to the graveside anyway.

Yet the main difference between the modern necromancer and the shaman of old is one of destination, for the spirits which are encountered by the adept as they seek this wisdom are very much a part of the waking world. There is no need to journey far for the dead, or what at first appears to be so, are all around.

This then is the realm of spirits which they seek. It is not beneath old oak roots or inside the grassy hills. It is in run down council houses, rambling mansions and biscuit factories. Supermarkets, caravans and foggy dawn streets. The local train network, buses and even their own home. All who still draw breath are swimming within a sea of drowned corpses, and largely unaware of the astral carrion in their midst.

In the shamanic worldview everything has a spirit. The trees and sky. Animals of all kinds. Even disease and pollution. The necromancer agrees, in theory, though tends to spend most of their time interacting with entities that no longer have a tether to the material plane in any real sense. Things that once were, but dwell only in memory now, awaiting a reason to be brought back to mind.

These then are not the intelligent essences of the landscape, but loose threads of what once dwelled within it. Frayed ends in the weave of fate, each with a unique story and some more willing to tell that tale than others. Teasing these ultimately fatal biographies out of the dead is not always necessary. Sometimes just acknowledging their presence is enough to make them seek company somewhere else.

Whether the necromancer considers them to be the actual souls of the departed who somehow got lost on the way to their allotted afterlife or as psychic manifestations of the mind that once was, the end result is largely the same. It is difficult to make either type leave the material realm. They rarely go into the light if ordered to do so. Short of dissolving them entirely the best that can be hoped for is that they are easily driven off.

The adept should also remember what side of the Veil that they live on. Theirs is a role which has as much to do with the living as those that no longer have that status. It is not a practice that occurs in a vacuum, at least not since its heyday in the Elizabethan Age when sorcerers used to be as self serving as lay preachers are today.

No, the modern art has seen a shift towards a more honest take on the profession. It's practitioners stand resolute as a mouthpiece for ancestral spirits and bulwark to stop the unseen from encroaching too far into human affairs. Gatekeepers and the gate all in one. Accelerated necromancy is a discipline that demands to be heard, shouted into the howling wind as it tries to give voice to the end that awaits all living things.

The new adept should be cautioned that such knowledge is not gained any faster by exploring the afterlife in a literal sense. There is no need to seek an early death to get there. The Reaper will be waiting at the allotted time, and does not wish to see her grim talents be called upon any earlier than fate originally intended.

No, there is much more to do within the bounds of the death current than simply joining the spirits where they dwell. The cultural significance of the actual act of dying, the folklore which has grown up around it and the depictions of loss it provides. Horror stories and tall tales. Personal journeys into the abyss. Fear of the unknown and the eventual release from pain. This is the heartbeat of the cemetery path.

So the stridently modern form that necromancy has taken during the early years of the 21st Century is far removed from the elitist cabal which seemed to cluster around such ideas in earlier times. This balance centred model is instead for the ghost hunters, mortuary workers, grief counsellors, witches and chaotes everywhere. All who would benefit from an acknowledgement of death in their lives are welcome.

Because ultimately the Veil is the vast, reflective pool that hides the eventual destination that all must visit regardless of wealth, class or actions. Heroes and villains both. All the while the accelerated necromancer is there at the bleeding edge of this otherwise solemn journey, peeping behind that curtain for kings and paupers alike. To know, to dare, to will, to tell the whole damn world. A rare and wondrous burden indeed.

Postmodern Concepts

Over the years I have developed my own cosmology to explain the weirder workings of the unseen. And surprisingly for some, the necromantic component does not require an actual soul in the classical sense to work. Perhaps a little on the stranger side for those who lack a background in memetics, what follows may still be of use when mapping out your own cemetery path.

Here you will find the concepts which underlie the spirit world within the accelerated necromancy model, though it has to also be understood that the tools and rituals later in this book are not exclusive to the following worldview. I am no ascended master, just a street level chaos magickian. And I have no desire to make others accept a set framework when gaining access to the tricks of my trade.

So call on the gods if you find value in the words, or seek out the energies inherent to graveyards for power should that be preferred. I designed this handbook to work just as well with the classical spirit model as my more information based one, and there is no need to slavishly join me in my admittedly postmodern paradigm just to get results. Do what you will, fellow adepts, and the Veil will be all the stronger for it.

Spiritual Digital

While some may scoff at an agnostic form of sorcery, in truth there is much to be gained from observing the supernatural from a position that robs those seemingly bizarre events of some of their impact. Preservation of sanity, for one, and continued personal autonomy when faced with the realisation that the world is a very strange place as well.

Because when interactions with the Veil are considered to be a part of the day to day functioning of the adept's life, as opposed to wildly bizarre supernatural incidents carrying a significant heavenly message, it is far easier to stay calm and formulate a balanced response in the rare cases where one is needed. And at that point the natural intersection between necromancy and chaos magick occurs.

That said, it is impossible to work within the unseen realms without some sort of framework that underlies all those odd interactions. Most would prefer the soul to remain an unknowable spiritual essence tied to their chosen religion, destined to either a grand afterlife or humble reincarnation once the current flesh is finally discarded. But as the following stridently digital model proves, it need not be so.

It argues that the core of our base reality is the void, the creative womb of Tiamat full to bursting with everything and nothing all at once. A wellspring of immanent information awaiting projection into the real via the billions upon billions of tiny calculations that underpin our not quite clockwork universe. The mind of a dead goddess expressing itself through children who have long forgotten she exists.

Some of these building blocks manifest as physical objects, others as core processes such as decay and entropy. Most important for human understanding of their reality are the conceptual ideas which govern the material world, even if many of these are purely arbitrary or in conflict with the actual facts. And if enough of the correct type of code coalesces around a given root it will become self aware.

In its purest form this inbuilt intelligence could be considered to be a combined by-product of context and experience. The first aspect identifies the reason for a given thing to exist, as well as its mechanics. The second describes how it is perceived by either itself or others once examined. And yes, this even applies to people, animals and anything else approaching sentience too.

Over time those base principles are bolstered by both refined definition and, should the conceptual basis find expression in material reality, interaction with other ideas too. No battle plan survives first contact with the enemy, and this is definitely true of the personality as it grows.

Each experience adds to the ever evolving bundle of information which defines who someone is and how they will react to future stimuli. The sense of self is born and bolstered as it is buffeted by the winds of culture. Everything the adept is has been created from layers of memory clothed in ever ageing flesh.

And if there is enough cohesion of will when the time comes then that basically digital soul crosses the Veil intact, returning to pure information in the same way that certain religions claim a reintegration with their overarching god. However, the program which has resulted from all that material experience remains autonomous, though not necessarily sentient, in its new immaterial home.

Heaven is a hard disk of sorts. An infinite storehouse of forms and function, ideas as the first building blocks of the universe and the last echoes of creation. It is not another plane of existence as much as it is a subsection of the very language that underpins reality itself, a chapter in the lexicon that is drawn from every time the void breathes a concept into existence. A quiet homecoming, back to the womb of Tiamat.

For the adept that continues to find value in the concept of reincarnation, then the non-physical side of the Veil could be thought of as something akin to a waiting room where those queueing up to be reborn are stored. If the preferred model is one that does not pay heed to the idea of a destined return, it could be considered a form of cold storage instead.

While comforting for some, it is hard to understand the overall point of a cyclic return to life after life. The actual mechanics of being redressed in flesh seem to rob the incoming personality of much of its former experience and leave only echoes of memory behind. This corruption of data is hardly an optimal method of reseeding of the mortal realm with prior knowledge, if that was ever the overarching goal in the first place.

And if karma and moral judgement are also removed from the equation there is even less reason to force an informational entity to return from Tiamat's womb to the material plane, as neither reward nor punishment are a driving factor either. No, when compared to each other the cold storage concept of the afterlife seems to carry far more weight from a purely process specific point of view.

Yes, this is admittedly reductionist. But seeing the other side of the Veil as some form of inert subatomic hard drive where all the individual personalities that were strong enough in their dying moments to remain coalesced are stored awaiting retrieval by a skilled practitioner solves a number of issues with the classical spirit based model of the afterlife.

Firstly, it addresses the lack of autonomy of the dead. This is not to say that some of those who have been freed from their flesh do not wander the world seeking interaction with the living of course. But they are a separate, conceptually lower form of entity known as a ghostform, and not a true representation of the collected information which made up the person as they died.

In general those stored on the other side of the Veil are inert bundles of information lacking the energetic spark to power any additional development. In this extra dimensional state they no longer accrete any further experience around their core context unless called upon by a wily and questioning adept through séance or ritual.

This leads directly to the second issue this almost digital vision of the afterlife answers. An intriguing aspect of communication between the realms of the living and the dead is the ambiguity created during such conversations. Incorrect answers are not necessarily a sign of dishonesty on the part of the medium, but instead an inescapable aspect of their still human nature.

Perhaps the adept who seeks to speak with the discarnate is not a direct conduit for the voices of the Veil, but a piece of fallible hardware reading that inert information and interpreting it through their own context and experience. And of course, the act of being accessed adds a record of that interaction to the digital footprint of the spirit being questioned too, thereby allowing their file to grow slightly in the process.

Finally, this paradigm also allows the priest or priestess of the Veil to discard the idea that those who have gone before are working behind the scenes to help the current crop of humanity evolve beyond their baser instincts. The dead are not actively gifted an understanding of all past and future events by virtue of their position outside of material space. If anything that is a hindrance and not a boon.

Long has necromancy toiled under such notions of the dead becoming minor gods in their own right based on their return to some form of all knowing and hopefully benevolent source. Yet that is proven to be wildly unrealistic when those entities are actually encountered by a dedicated medium who seeks them out in hopes of achieving enlightenment through those frankly dubious answers.

That is not to say that a spirit has to stop its growth when consigned to the hard drive of history. But the act of collecting more experience around their contextual core would require the program that they have become to find the energy to enter into a read/write state, and this is usually only possible when someone from the material realm finds a good enough reason to ritually visit the womb of Tiamat in the first place.

Ghostforms

A pseudo-entity mentioned earlier in my underlying necromantic cosmology, the ghostform is an accidental by-product of a strong enough personality crossing the Veil. While comparatively rare if viewed against the balance of all those who pass without any complications, it is also the most common spirit that people will actively encounter in their day to day lives.

Of course, as with the entire digital afterlife model the exclusivity of these pseudo-entities in the broader haunted house mythology can be discarded by those who follow a more traditional spiritual path. That said, the idea that not everything bumping away in the night was once a complete human soul has led me to some very illuminating interactions when the lights go out.

Regardless of either age or adherents, all religions are destined to run up against the problem of the Veil at some point. Indeed the many ways of explaining this mortal step towards the unreal world actively defines the majority of those paths in the cultural landscape. Even just a cursory look at the taboos around gaining access to whichever final destination they prefer will easily prove that point.

For too many in power the afterlife is little more than a cruel method of getting the downtrodden to sacrifice everything of value during their fleshy incarnation in service of what might await them after that now broken body can give no more. This is inherently unfair, yet from the earliest civilisations to now has been broadly accepted as truth.

It is impossible to carve away the more judgemental aspects of those systems without invalidating much of their scripture. The only cure is to remove the idea of a semi-physical afterlife wholesale and replace it with one born of stored information awaiting access by a suitably skilled necromancer instead.

While that adept could hail from any of a thousand spiritual backgrounds, or indeed none, what happens once the flesh is discarded remains their ever present concern. And an enduring interest in seeking out those discarnate entities can lead to some surprising revelations.

Most people go quietly into that darkest of nights, be it via the classical release of their soul at the point of death or the archiving of the information that made them who they were should the digital model championed by accelerated necromancers be preferred.

Yet not all that whispers incoherently as it climbs the stairs to the attic is a wondering spirit in the accepted sense. In a universe that allows for the presence of foreign anomalies such as the Faerie or man made gods like Cthulhu, ghosts are just as likely to be projected mental energy as anything else.

Unlike the more widely accepted but originally fictitious stone tape theory the ghostform is an autonomous being free from ties to either location or time of year. Those more inattentive manifestations are usually either echoes or shards, and of little note to those who walk the cemetery path outside of an interesting side quest on a ghost hunt.

While the science surrounding death is understandably more interested in preventing it from occurring ahead of time or seeking answers as to why and how that spark of life was ultimately extinguished after the fact, limited research has been conducted into the final moments of biological existence.

Yet studies in laboratory animals do seem to show a spike in neural activity around the time of death, as the brains struggles to try and right a rapidly sinking ship with most of the crew dead and a massive bleeding hole in the hull. It is in this phase of the dying process that the ghostform is born.

In higher order animals such as large mammals, and of course humans too, pain seems to ease in those final seconds. There is some evidence that all available endorphins are released en-masse to ease this violent stress, probably leading to near death hallucinations and the classic tunnel of light scenario as reported by the few who died and then lived to tell the tale afterwards.

For those who are not lucky enough to be coming back, those endorphins usher in the final moments of their mortal experience. As the nervous system stutters into inertia and oxygen deprivation begins to kill their braincells that final burst of activity occurs. Just as with the laboratory animals, the brain refuses to power down without a last ditch effort to fight back.

An attempt to remember who they were, to fight for coalescence as their whole world dissolves. What they enjoyed, time spent with loved ones, the family they will now be leaving behind and those they hope to see on the other side. But also secret addictions and lusts unfulfilled. Good and bad with no gods to judge them. Freedom at last.

All that the person is, their memories, wants and needs are folded into an infinitely dense package as the synapses around that super dense sphere of information begin to burn to ash. Should they be strong enough in their sense of self this is what passes beyond the Veil to be placed in cold storage alongside their ancestors, though said digital future is not guaranteed.

It is far from a perfect process, and occasionally the transfer springs a metaphysical leak. Anyone who is familiar with the concept of the void in chaos magick will recognise this intense focus as a gateway to manifestation, and that is indeed what seems to happen in some rare, but notable cases.

Thus the out of control mental stress, as well as the desire to retain a sense of self, can force the birth of a fractured and malformed thoughtform based loosely on the contents of the brain during shutdown. A ghost in all but name, this pseudo-entity is the reason why certain locations and people are seen as haunted. Perhaps possessed as well, though that is veering dangerously towards Satanic Panic territory.

Astral parasites of far greater power and intelligence than the echoes which are usually encountered by the living, these often malevolent and worryingly uninhibited collections of scrambled code are capable of causing serious damage, at least on a mental level. More so than the grief and fear which sustains their lesser brethren they instead seek to feed on the desires which drove their real world counterpart.

Be they once hidden or openly experienced during life, these pseudo-entities will have no earthly inhibitions to stop them indulging that hunger ravenously once a host is found. And yes, their greater remaining intellect, stronger will and ability to communicate in something approaching an actual language pushes them far beyond the lowly echoes and non sentient shards in pure manipulative skill.

Regardless of whether the idea of an exclusively digital spirit world is part of the adept's overarching paradigm or a more mixed model where regular soul based spirits also exist in the wild as well is adopted, the concept of ghostform does answer some nagging questions which plague the more classical take on the topic. Firstly, it solves the glaring issue of why the dead seem to be missing something when encountered.

They act fundamentally damaged and mentally incoherent, chasing the same experiences again and again, as if they were lost in some form of almost chemical educed haze and hungry for any action that will feed their single driving emotion. Which of course was the state of the mind they were born from during that organ's endorphin fuelled shutdown.

Secondly it also clarifies why ghosts are very often hobbled by factors such as injury, disease or long term disability. This flies in the face of most mainstream spiritual systems which claim the soul is returned to a pure state when the imperfect flesh is discarded. Religions must promise such a release from pain, of course, otherwise no one would endure that burden in service of those ideals while alive.

Yes, that may in fact be a true side effect of crossing the Veil. But these pseudo-entities are not the soul in the classical sense, and so are not bound by those expectations. If the mind was instead fixated on the damage to the mortal shell, be it a fact of their life or a gory manifestation of their death, that will be the shape the tulpa finds itself in once born. Torture and mutilation carried forward for all eternity. A literal Hell.

Finally it may explain why certain groups such as the overly religious or staunchly atheistic do not seem to be as strongly represented in paranormal folklore as those who were somewhere in between and likely undecided about their final destination. Seeing neither their deity of choice or welcome mechanistic oblivion as shutdown approaches, these are the potential ghostform catalysts.

And based on the general attitude of most wondering spirits when encountered in the wild those manifestations seem to be heavily skewed towards those who would have lacked the time to make their peace and embrace either the journey to the afterlife or sweet, numbing oblivion.

Thus the brief internal struggle, intense focus on the sense of self and possible brain damage lead to the generation of a deeply flawed and potentially dangerous thought form. One loosed to roam the material side of the Veil and feed on the energy of the living in a doomed attempt to satiate a desire for mortal experience that they can never escape. Smart enough to be a wily hunter, but too dumb to escape its own vices.

It is these pseudo-entities which plague the séance rooms and Ouija boards the world over, each a babbling and incoherent informational clone unaware that they are not the person they thought they were. No matter the evidence it is impossible to make them see that, of course, and perhaps it is unfair to even try.

While it may be theoretically possible to force such a thoughtform into existence at the time of death, to create a revenant of sorts for altruistic means such as watching over the adept's decedents or a particularly loved institution, the odds are still against it causing anything but trouble once it has been loosed upon the world. This is all an accident, a by-product of the human need to stay alive when faced with annihilation.

So it may not be the spirits of the once living wondering the material plane seeking solace from those who still have a heartbeat. If ghostform theory is correct then their hyper fixated mental children do instead, albeit without realising they are simply the Jungian shadow given license to roam freely. An instrument of sorrow imprinted with the animal at the core of the person who once was, and a grave mistake in the making.

Regardless of the details, as the population grows so do the number of potential catalysts waiting to give birth to a monster that few can see and even less resist. The necromancer will carry that burden, keep the realms of the living and the dead apart as much as possible. They are few, true. But the Veil gives those on the cemetery path the strength to keep putting one foot in front of the other.

Haunting Yourself

We all have an inner primitive. A bundle of core wants and secret desires, this Jungian shadow is just waiting to be free of the cultural rules imposed upon it by its imprisonment within flesh. Once free to roam the world, walking along the corpse ways of the city and acting on their whims without fear of consequences, these astral parasites can even be deadly.

As a necromancer I am not immune from the danger of my potential ghostform becoming just as nasty as anyone else's once I cross the Veil. Though by working towards a truce with those aspects of myself which hide behind this otherwise understanding smile, allowing them some small purchase within my day to day life, I hope that darkness will be far less pronounced after my death.

The folklore surrounding the spirit world has a heavy bias towards spooky old castles or timber framed historical buildings. While this may have more to do with telling tall tales by the fireside as opposed to provable supernatural activity, less seems to have been said about the role that individuals play in the haunted landscape. Because people, as well as places, can be just as infested with things unseen.

Parasitic pseudo-entities who have developed a taste for the dopamine rush of experiences they once enjoyed in life after death should have put an end to such indulgences, they are attracted to the same in the still living. And so begin to feed on the energies released within their carrier's nervous system during those actions, whispering all the while that just one more hit is what the victim needs to feel better.

Unless their secret vice was one of causing fear, of course, in which case they can feed on just about anyone prone to jump at a loud noise or slamming door. Children are also not immune from this sort of attention, even though they have yet to develop any notable vices which can be latched on to. Theirs is the innocence of youth, and this seems to attract imaginary friends of all shapes and kinds. Rarely a good thing.

Shadow work has become something of a hot topic in Neopagan circles in recent years. Important, but potentially dangerous if not undertaken with suitable care, there are a number of books which approach the process of integrating the darker side of the personality from an almost apologetic angle, fearing those aspects of themselves that want and need and lust. All are simply ghostforms in the making, nothing more.

Any who stand alone in the liminal spaces at the edges of the unseen world will realise that there are already enough people out there cursing the day the adept was born for the mostly taboo actions undertaken while walking the cemetery path anyway. As such little can be gained by deconstructing a perfectly serviceable ego at the behest of new age authors who likely have their own secrets well hidden too.

The accelerated necromancer eschews such blatant self loathing, choosing to shape their soul through more direct means. That is their right as vessels for the death current and chosen of the Veil. This bundle of repressed needs and carnal desires is not ignored or even integrated but instead applauded, given a role within their mortal lives that befits the inherent raging power that it represents.

All magick comes from the ego, and reflects desires both accepted and repressed as it finds expression within the waking world. Aspects which are viewed with suspicion and hidden unduly will likely out when a related ritual is completed anyway, leading to a subtle twisting of the outcome towards facilitating those deeper drives. Lust of result in a literal sense, able to do truly strange things if left unchecked.

Of course when examined in a thorough way the shadow side of the personality can be useful. Accelerated necromancers should seek to personify this internalised complex of rage and shame, before putting it to work as a familiar. There is power in pain, and breaking away a part of the inner landscape to grant this hidden lord of shadows their own fiefdom allows them enough autonomy to develop and grow.

And all that is required to do this is a journal, pen and an hour or so at night. The first stage is by far the most troubling for those who find solace for the suppression of their inner drives through social acceptance and either religious or cultural commandments. Every night before bed a paragraph or two is created, not a diary which lists events but a rumination upon the feelings which were generated by them instead.

Honesty with oneself is key here, and for those who worry about such frankness of desire being found by others perhaps a digital document would be better, hidden on a hard drive and password protected away from prying eyes, Regardless of format chosen, it is the stream of consciousness evaluation of the day which matters, both positive and negative, fanciful and grounded in personal truth.

After a week the adept should become more comfortable with the blatant honesty that this process requires, and after a month laying down those passionate or rage filled sentences will be second nature. The desired result is not to act upon those words, there has been enough coverage of disgruntled employees attacking their work place or stalking a coworker in the news. Self discipline is key above all else here.

For those who also keep a dream diary as part of their regular occult practice these insights into the deepest reaches of the subconscious, wrapped up in allegory and symbolism as they are, can be cross referenced to provide corroborating evidence as well. Of course the adept would be unlikely to base the plans they make in the waking world upon their nocturnal one. Same should be said for their nightly journaling too.

No, the next stage of the process once enough of these pages have collected guiltily by lamplight is to go through them and find the common themes. There may be several, each supported by hundreds of interrelated sentences which point to the hidden face of the ego. A few of the Jungian archetypes will likely appear in the ink, and can be noted for future use.

Of these, the Shadow is the most relevant to the process which the accelerated necromancer is undertaking. Immoral and inferior, this dark side of the psyche is the Mr Hyde to their Dr. Jekyll, and can find support from the Trickster, a childish and gratification obsessed facet of the personality that cruelly takes what it wants with no heed to the cost. These should both sound familiar to those who deal with ghostforms.

The adept need not despair, however, because Jung saw the potential for good in the collective unconscious as well, and left a space for the Hero. This is the human drive to good for its own sake, to overcome evil and leave the world a better place. For those who have excelled at some intellectual or worldly task, the Wise Old Man can also add their positivity, as long as it does not represent a detachment from worldly concerns.

The adept teases out the sentences in their journals which, for good or ill, fall under the sway of the four archetypes noted above, accepting any imbalance towards the negative which may be on display. For those who wish to delve even deeper into the works of Carl Jung, the other archetypes that he outlined, such as the Animus or Anima can also be explored, though are not necessary for the simple process outlined below.

Once enough context has been journaled, the necromancer will know at what point this is as the words start to lose their raw and needful ache, they are transferred to a separate document under the archetypal headings which make the most sense. Thus intensely personal expressions of the Shadow, Trickster, Hero and perhaps even the Wise Old Man will fill those pages, and provide a doorway into the psychic landscape of the adept.

Yes, those out of context sentences truly do represent a window into the state of the soul, a look at the future of the ghostform which resides within the mind, and a roadmap of sorts that will allow the necromancer to stand alone as a sovereign being free at last to either be true to their core nature or try to correct the parts of their ship that might be causing it to slowly sink.

By reading those excerpts while holding an admittedly initially one sided internal dialogue with whatever is bubbling down beneath the surface of the deep mind, examining those drives through fantasy and visualisation, it will soon become apparent that the shadow side of the ego has its own voice, and is all too willing to communicate once it realises that it will not face instant attack for doing so.

Over a long enough period this discussion also becomes second nature and a distinct persona will coalesce around those sarcastic and sour thoughts, allowing it to add its own input to the already complicated memetic soup of internalised discussions that the adept experiences when going about their day. It might even develop a shape bordering on the totemic, or appear as a spirit guide like with the mediums of old.

This, then, is how an accelerated necromancer haunts themselves. By accessing the ghostform which resides within their own repressed desires they become almost immune to the attentions of the similar but long dead astral parasites which are looking for a free lunch among the tombstones. Such jealous pseudo-entities rarely like to share a meal, and this allows the adept a safer walk along their cemetery path as a result.

For those who prefer a more classical take on the concept of soul and afterlife, and find little of use in the ghostform theory, the journaling and self reflection techniques described here are still a viable way to gain insight into those core drives that many would hide. Regardless of the paradigm chosen the underlying landscape of the deep mind will still have real world effects, and should be treated with care.

Current Concerns

The overarching narrative device within my personal occult paradigm is the idea of currents. Memetic building blocks of all esoteric and even social concepts, they describe a fast fall towards the centre of a given topic while hitting every point of note on the way down.

Useful to internalise vastly complex forces on a manageable mental scale, this piecemeal method of approaching the theories that underpin the workings of the universe in starkly human terms also feeds back into the conceit that information forms the underlying structure of reality as we know it.

What follows is an attempt to explain exactly what one of these currents would look like in relation to death and decay, hopefully as succinctly as possible. And of course the framework for containing such multifaceted hyperobjects can be applied to anything else mankind chose to name and claim since language first became a thing too.

Understanding The Death Current

While most would be happy to work within a paradigm that reflects the classic spirit model of magick, the accelerated necromancer is not tied to such an old fashioned framework. Indeed, while they often talk of the death current as a driving force for the more ritualised aspect of the craft, it is in truth very different from what most would assume.

Far from just being some nebulous mystical wellspring that flows freely from the jagged gateways of the underworld the term actually refers to an all encompassing metanarrative that includes sour reverence, wilting emotion, primal desire and so much more besides. Because the memetic bundle which surrounds the actual concept of the end of life is vastly more important than any individual passing ever could be.

Yes, the death current does include the cold entropic energy encountered in places associated with decomposition and transit across the Veil. But the electrical hum of an open grave or tortured friction spewing forth from sites of mass slaughter are but a small part of what truly makes up the necromancer's sphere of influence.

Meaning. Context. Information. Loss. Since the first burials thousands of years ago this massive memetic bundle has been slowly growing. Bolstered by taboo and reverie, sorrow and acceptance, ever expanding as more and more people were either lowered into the embrace of the soil or left to rot among the corpses of their enemies above it.

And as every culture crawled towards its apex they added their own funerary practices and battlefield horrors to the cultural record, as well as the underworlds and heavens which made the most sense at the time. A sweeping and nonsensical narrative that survives to this day, albeit in fragmentary form.

Gods and goddesses watched over the population, each a shard of longing that scratched away at the imaginations of those left to mourn until they were finally wailed into existence through floods of tears. Hecate. Charon. Morrigan. Hades and Hel herself. Too many spirits to name, too few remembered as history marches ever forwards along its own cemetery path towards the eventual end of all things.

Yet the pressure they created on the human psyche was not completely forgotten. Nothing ever is, not when language conspires to keep old ideas alive through layers of association. And thus the bundle of information grows ever larger, swallowing both the dead and those who deal with them alike.

Animals such as the noble wolf or capricious raven were given the role of psychopomp by virtue of their associations with carrion, before angels quickly replaced those earthen spirits as something crudely alien from on high. And once those interlopers arrived the right to bargain with the guides to the underworld for a second chance was gone too. No games of chess or dice with the Reaper. Just acceptance or Hell.

Relegated to myths and stories, those early expressions of death and decay were instead deified through folklore, becoming forever bonded to the Veil through the traditions which survived the Abrahamic religions and their assassination of imagination. Words have power. The adept would do well to remember that.

So the term current, in the context of modern practice, does not just describe a simple flow of energy, or even a power source. Those who work with these bundles of information may indeed choose to draw upon the necromantic essence that pools at certain locations, but that cool background hum is only one fragment of bone within a metaphorical sea of corpses all awaiting exploration.

Because the true priest or priestess of the Veil must realise above all else that the actual idea of death is way more powerful than the act of dying itself. Treating the concept of magickal currents as little better than mental shorthand for the act of drawing energy from sea, sky or forest is to drastically undermine the true beauty of the mystical within the physical.

Far more than just a tool, the current forms an entire worldview, a vast drowning pool of interrelated topics that the necromancer must descend into so that they can rise again with enough hard won knowledge to make a difference in the world. Weaponised memetics, for those who would admit to the existence of such a thing, or the shamanic journey to rebirth if that explanation is preferred.

While not strictly alive, the death current is potentially sentient by virtue of the sheer amount of information which has coalesced around the topic since both language and empathy became human considerations. It finds expression through all actions that result in extinction, though surprisingly the preservation of life is also a part of that solemn conceptual framework too.

After all, the Reaper smiles as each new life is birthed into the world, watching silently as it ages to its prime before the descent into sickness and old age take hold. Nothing pleases her more than hearing of those triumphs and tribulations, pride and sorrow as she leads the person from the cemetery path to the waiting gates of the Veil. A full life and good death is all the devotion she really needs.

Of course she is not a deity, more an almost elemental expression of the eventual decay at the end of all things. Perhaps to understand the sheer vastness of the death current in relation to the smaller gods and goddesses which have coalesced around its blackened heart, or the insignificance of the necromancer within this paradigm, an analogy may be useful.

Tiamat. Mesopotamian mother of the gods who through her death laid the foundations for the birth of mankind. Embodiment of the swirling and primordial salt sea. Rent in two by the storm god Marduk, her body would be cast to the heavens to form the milky way and downward to create the very land upon which the human race now stands.

A single creation story among many, but one of the few which involves the death of a primordial super god of immeasurable divine power who through their defeat or sacrifice goes on to lay the physical foundations for billions of material worlds.

Again, words have power here. Choosing to refer to the swirling everything and nothing at the core of creation as the womb of Tiamat is not just a literary conceit. As the foundation stone of the Earth in humankind's earliest surviving cultural narratives, and one which may be even older than the Mesopotamian people themselves, it certainly has the weight of history on its side.

Regardless of naming conventions the overall analogy stands true. As a result the death current can be viewed as something akin to Tiamat in her role as unwilling founder of the land of men, a vastly overarching idea which stands apart from the immortal gods it spawns and short lived humans it gives context. The canvas upon which all else is painted, for good or ill, until that vital pigment is eventually exhausted.

All currents are unknowable as a complete and total whole. The entire gamut of emotions, reasons for decay, disease and relief from pain. No necromancer could ever hope to bond with it completely, even crossing the Veil does not grant that boon. As such, the adept will find themselves specialising in the aspects of that information bundle which drive their research on a purely personal level instead.

In that context another analogy proves to be useful. The viral spread of a specific property in popular culture actually requires the creation of various additional stories or concepts by the associated fandoms outside of the cannon central narrative. Every theory becomes apocrypha, question heresy, yet the more people who approach a topic with interest the more power it gains.

All the while that original story, be it a comic book series, video game trilogy or film franchise, sails upon this ever expanding sea of unofficial content, with viewpoints and cliques forming shortly after. Soon subfandoms and spin-offs abound. Of such a human desire to understand and belong are religions made, because sad to say even untrue words have power too.

Returning to the death current as a force it can be assumed this ever approaching annihilation as a constant antithesis to the gift of life is the cannon original narrative. Set in stone and immutable, eventually everything will end, people, planets and even universes all brought to a hard stop as time itself accepts oblivion.

Mankind's earliest ancestors likely howled against the winds when they first realised that inescapable truth. And from that deep rooted need to somehow name and explain that mounting terror of oblivion the gods, goddesses, psychopomps, spirits and funerary practices were formed. Perhaps the Reaper in the guise we now recognise her first coalesced at that instant too, though she will of course never tell.

This, then, is the death current. A human invention as old as the perception of absence itself, a tool to aid beings painfully low down the cosmic scale in trying to name a concept so vast as to be ultimately unfathomable. Entropy, decay and annihilation as core processes are in there, of course, but obfuscated by the millennia rich tapestry that cultures both recent and long forgotten wove around those ideas.

Oh, there is vast power in words. Concepts too. The necromancer is most at home when further tailoring those historical threads into a personal narrative that inches ever closer to the core truth which underpins their meaning. There are no masters upon the cemetery path, only adepts at different stages of their journey. And none among them have forgotten that their ultimate destination can only ever be the Veil.

How The Death Current Mixes

As a heady combination of entropic elemental energy and accreted meaning, the death current actually exists within the same cultural melting pot as various other ideas of equal complexity. And as can be imagined, there is some intermingling and overlap of all of these within the modern mind.

As an urban adept I have personally worked with the following blended essences on numerous occasions over the years, and while the results have not always been reliable they were usually interesting. Your location and skill with different magickal systems may render some of these more effective than others, though all are worth a try at least once.

No current exists in a vacuum. Like any other fundamental aspect of the human condition the idea of death as a cultural force regularly brushes up against other equally vast and overarching ideas. And on the fringes of this meeting there will be a melding of sorts, a blending of form and function which may well allow for entirely new esoteric worldviews to take shape.

The accelerated necromancer should attempt to explore all viable blends, even those that are not listed here. Everything, no matter how large or long lived, will cease to do exactly that at some point in its future. As a fundamental process of decay when matter is subjected to time, death itself becomes a rare universal law which underpins most other structures, even as a counterpoint.

Of course ideas can die too. Many have due to the actions of the prevailing intelligentsia throughout history. But as has been seen with the esoteric religious movements that flower in secret and then rot under public scrutiny even just the knowledge that a thing once existed may be all that is needed to allow fresh seeds to be planted that will one day bloom again.

Biophilic Blend
By far the easiest of the combined concepts to see in the wild, a necromancer need only sit beneath the shaded trees in their local graveyard to feel the shivering warmth welling up from the plants around them. Nature as a militant force which drives plants and animals to reclaim the urban landscape is represented almost everywhere, of course, but rarely in such overwhelming profusion as when inside cemetery bounds.

Considering that most cities lack any green spaces outside of parks or rubbish choked patches of derelict land the sites where cultures hide the dead to ease the consciences of the living become a fall back option for those wishing to understand Gaia's pain while stuck within larger human sprawls. Gardens of the dead in more ways than one, all ripe for harvest.

To know what was lost when mankind decided to use concrete and glass to hide their lives from her gaze, a willing adept need only watch the brambles choke a once grand tomb or wildflowers spread across the otherwise nondescript potters field. This is of course all the easier should the graveyard also be designated a reserve where the plants are allowed to grow freely for most of the year.

As Gaia works at imperceptible speeds to take back what was hers something approaching an instinctual understanding of deep time begins to emerge. The adept should realise that the average human lifespan is inconsequential compared to the ever crawling, constantly reclaiming natural world, while shouldering the burden that the damage they do now will echo long after their bones are dust beneath the soil.

Notable rituals to undertake within those ivy clad boundaries are acts of devotion, such as a quiet litter picking or tidying of a segment of graves to grant a deeper knowledge of the state in which they one day too may lie. This would also work as self imposed penance for upsetting the balance or otherwise stepping outside the seven necromantic laws without just cause too.

Alternatively, the drawing of stored energy which pulses beneath the gnarled and usually vandalised bark of the aged trees growing like wooden ghouls over the older graves can reenergise even the most exhausted adept. Particularly ancient ones may have grown into broken dryads, a creature born of the friction caused when Gaia and the Reaper find common ground in the same place.

This then could be considered the biophilic blend. Nature and death as a mixed force, the stillborn yet somehow vibrantly alive love-child of two concepts that would at first appear to be diametrically opposed. Perhaps best described as a sluggish flow of grim reclamation, much can be achieved when the accelerated necromancer chooses to dedicate part of their practice towards the green world itself.

Mechanistic Blend

A more difficult essence to work with, the rise of automation and the digital may at first appear to be at odds with the idea of magick in general. Yet just as with any other tool that the adept uses to change the swing of the pendulum in their favour, neither machine nor program can be considered free from the ever present influence of death.

Swords, spears, axes and even slings. Stone weapons through to modern rifle cartridges and everything in between. Torture devices and satanic mills. Fleshy cogs in a soulless machine. Innovation has always had a bloody tinge to it, a need to defend and improve warped into domination for sadistic fun and shareholder profit.

The technological current as a whole will always be tarnished by this association, especially when even the most altruistic of medical devices would have been tested upon those who did not make it through the procedure alive. That said, the necromancer has little to gain by abandoning the material world wholesale while those around them are instead granted its dubious boons.

Moderation and compassion towards nature are key when striving to maintain the balance, and green technologies should be embraced where possible to help lighten the ever increasing load on the world. More Technogaianism than solarpunk, this viewpoint accepts that industrialisation has caused harm, but strives to evolve beyond that point to one where it is also the method by which the world is healed as well.

From a ritualistic point of view the accelerated necromancer should embrace their inner fabricator. Crafting magickal tools from found objects not only brings the cost and carbon footprint of those objects down but also lessens the chance that third-world sweatshop labour had been used in their creation. This is especially important when the adept can feel the blood of those who were mistreated on everything they buy.

Additionally, seances and other more mediumistic operations can benefit from audio and video of the deceased person on loop in the background, or if footage of the target is unavailable a general suite of electronic voice phenomenon can be set to shuffle instead. Even ghost photos, regardless of their dubious origin, can help set the stage for some late night shenanigans.

So in this meeting of the necromantic and the digital the mechanistic blend finds its most vibrant expression. With the online world becoming something akin to a second astral plane, and holograms of famous musicians blurring the line between life and death, the necromancer would do well to embrace the tools of modernity while keeping one eye on the natural balance that industrialisation may disrupt.

Urbanistic Blend

As rich a source of subliminal information as the very idea of the built environment itself, geography plays a vital role in how the adept will go on to approach their practice. Social status, overarching religious views, even the languages spoken will be based on the city or state that they call home. This, then, is the urban current.

Plague pits, martyr pyres, old meat markets and slaughterhouses. Castle dungeons and battlefields. Serial killers in suburbia and suicides within inner city estates. From the earliest habitation to the current cookie cutter investment flats, the living city is a massive open sore just oozing untold death and hardship into the streets that criss-cross its bulk.

While the map is never the territory beauty can be found in the way that architects hammer out their trade upon Gaia's unwilling flesh. Layers of water pipes, internet cables, sewers and transit tunnels. Power and telephone lines above, basements and bunkers below. The individual strata of the city as chakras burrowing from the earth to the sky. Sutras in the soil.

Actively mythologising places like London or New York is not a new concept. Many novels exist to do just that. Yet the adept should remember that they have the same ability regardless of the size of their home village or town. And of course the first waypoints which spring to mind for those of a necrogeographic persuasion are churchyards or cemeteries, the very spirit of place written large on every gravestone.

Ritualistic endeavours centred around claiming those sites of burial and using them as an anchor point for the adept's journey into the wider city can lead to a better understanding of the area in which they live, as well as focal points to call that human history back into the cold light of day. And the dead, metaphorically piled high under the paving slabs and tarmac streets, are ever present.

Outside of the churchyard, long walks among the less travelled alleyways and concrete gulleys of the adept's home town will further boost this sense of place while also granting them the time to reflect upon how that urban sprawl taints their view of the world. Particularly reckless necromancers can even attempt to claim a whole city, though few will likely have the presence of mind to succeed.

And here, as the dead tower blocks and living history merge, the urbanistic blend rushes like an icy river beneath the surface. Some have argued in the past that cities are cannibalistic, feeding upon the toil of those who all too quickly grow, age and then die within its homes. This is mostly true, and the necromancer would do well to remember the fate of those who walked those smog choked streets in ages past.

The Many Faced Reaper

When questioned about the more memetic aspects of my chaos magick tinged take on necromancy the identity of the Reaper herself inevitably comes up. Most consider this to be a stridently male spirit, robed in tattered black and bony hand curled around a warped and rusty scythe.

An image that undoubtedly carries a vast reservoir of coalesced thought around it since at least the late Medieval age, but one that I do not actually agree with. In my experience she is more mother goddess than stern step-father, though my conclusions as to who she actually is may surprise you.

It is only normal for those of a necromantic persuasion to cast a reverent eye upon the goddesses of death as part of their practice. Such supplication to the manifestations of divinity within the cultural landscape is an expected aspect of some occult disciplines, though the true adept should instead attempt to remain apart from this forced compliance wherever possible.

The final journey across the Veil is one of quiet solitude after all, undertaken without friends or fanfare and ignored by the majority of chthonic deities unless they are promised to an underworld kingdom over which that entity holds sway. Everyone dies alone, even when released from their burdensome flesh in the company of others. An uncomfortable, but honest, truth.

No, the chthonic gods of classical mythology have very little role in that interplay between humanity and the Reaper. But who the solemn yet smiling entity that haunts the accelerated necromancer's dreams and whispers of future oblivion to the uninitiated actually is remains a difficult question to answer.

It is human nature to name and claim the world around them. The mind, being little better than a physical expression of bundled information, abhors unanswered questions. Plot holes and loose ends in a tale will drive men to madness as they seek the solution. Words have power, after all, and incantations to explain away the shadows hold more than most.

So perhaps the Reaper is Persephone, the wronged goddess whose cyclic imprisonment in the underworld and release back to the lands of men is at the core of the necromancer's broken wheel of the year. Tied as she is to the idea of death and rebirth, hers would be a suitable mask to lay upon the reaper's smiling face. But no, she is not who the adept should seek.

Hekate could just as easily fulfil the role, grand and stern Titaness and keeper of the crossroads, it is to her that the majority of modern witches pray. An amalgamation of many local cult deities from the classical era, such as Enodia and Melinoë, her far reach and accepted role as a psychopomp would be a worthy fit for the Reaper's cowl. Yet she is also the wrong choice.

Or maybe it is Demeter, Persephone's mother who holds the mantle. A goddess of the harvest who denies the gods their tribute in retaliation for her daughter's forced marriage to Hades, her sorrow and anger is the reason why winter comes and then eases to allow an all too brief summer. A good fit for the Reaper's sorrow, but she is not the one.

Santa Muerte is a strong candidate of course. A prominent figure in Latin American culture, her overt veneration goes back at least to the 18th Century, perhaps even longer in secret. Saint Death has achieved a meteoric rise to prominence through both the folk Catholic and Neopagan paradigms in recent years and would be a perfect fit for the Reaper's aura of quiet calm. It is not her, though.

Travelling even further back the goddess Ereshkigal holds court over the Mesopotamian underworld, the lands of dry dust and murky water which were thought to await all mortals, both good and bad. She has a cold countenance, vengeful towards the few who would challenge her power whether they be fellow gods or lowly mortals. A good fit for the Reaper's seeming callousness, yet in truth not the answer either.

Demonesses then. The mighty and lustful Lilith, holding as she does the revered position as the first of the Abrahamic God's creations to stand up to that draconian and ultraconservative essence in defence of her rights as a sovereign feminine being. Supposedly now the slayer of babies and queen of the succubi, hers would be a very apt fit for the Reaper's cooling touch. But again, the role is not a good enough fit.

The answer might lie in thinking about the topic from a much broader perspective, then. Tiamat, for example, primal goddess who according to the Babylonian epic of creation became the very flesh of the Earth could be walking among her children and taking them on their final journey back to her womb to be reborn. A rehabilitation of an otherwise chaotic force perhaps, though hers is not the Reaper's scythe.

Fiction has its fair share of archetypes that can be harnessed to answer the question of course. Death of the Endless, the smart, upbeat yet soulful psychopomp created by Neil Gaiman and Mike Dringenberg for Vertigo Comics is an exceptional representation of the Reaper's heart. But while without a doubt the most relatable entity on this list those literary origins seem to exclude her from the race before it has even begun.

All that merely scratched the surface. The number of potential goddesses who could lay claim to the role of Reaper, fictional or otherwise, is as broad as human imagination. Yet the truth of the matter is that there are only candidates here, potential answers that cluster around the death current like teeth in a bleeding and skeletal maw. And therein lies the twist in this otherwise all too human tale.

Death as an end to life existed long before mankind or the deities they birthed into existence around them to help name and claim the wider world. Early hominids died of course. Small mammals and before that dinosaurs too. Single cell organisms within the vast bubbling primordial oceans consumed each other or succumbed to old age.

That is the impossibly long grip that the Reaper has on this world, though it would take the rise of both self reflection and language to gift her that name. It must be remembered that this is a cosmic mechanism that transcends species and place entirely, so only the intersection of that force with the human race grants her a form which the adept can strive to recognise.

Even assigning her gender in the binary sense is a waste of time, though many who walk the cemetery path will attest to the oddly feminine energy that she seems to exude when encountered in dream or reverie. It may be a leap of faith, but this strangely maternal, almost mother goddess association seems to ring true.

The accelerated necromancer, skilled as they are in memetics, understand that words are not just the description of a thing but also a way to bring that concept or object to heel. To know the name of the demon is to gain control over it. And there lies not only the inherent power of language but also the reason why it is so dangerous. A lie is no different to the truth when spreading through the cultural aggregate.

And so the answer is as obvious as it is oblique. She is all of the goddesses mentioned above and none. Those are human names, cultural memes, a mere attempt to pacify the inevitable end of all things by granting it a recognisable shape.

The Reaper is a true paradox of meaning, an amalgamation of every idea which mankind pinned on that already ancient and inevitable function of decay rising from the action of time within the material universe. The necromancer, accelerated or otherwise, must understand that these shards of identity are just facets of a much bigger uncut whole.

Because regardless of the adept's chosen philosophy, it is fundamental forces and not deities which will oversee the end of their lives. Far from obfuscating the truth this openness to the idea that her presence within the already expanded boundaries of the accelerated necromancer's death current fuelled world will empower them to work with whichever goddess mask they are most comfortable with.

Perhaps the early hominids had a name for her, now long forgotten. Predating the modern iteration of the death current, created as it is from collected human experience overlaid on the processes of age and decay, the Reaper can be engaged with as any of the names she has been gifted over thousands of years of human civilisation, or indeed none. That much at least the adept can claim to control.

It is not that there is no right answer, but that there were never any wrong ones either. Regardless of the various masks she has worn through the centuries, many now lost to time along with the people who once gifted her those titles, the Reaper still exists on the sidelines of the mundane world. There she sits with a warm and understanding smile, waiting to take all who live on their final journey home.

Sorcerers of any discipline like to think of themselves as all knowing, and to admit that the best they can do is give fleeting faces to such a fundamental force of unravelling is to concede that they have secrets yet to learn. But such willingness to admit that the answer is extremely complex and perhaps also a little counter-intuitive can only aid the necromancer in their journey towards a better understanding of the Veil.

BOOK TWO

Starting To See

The initial steps taken upon the cemetery path are for many the most difficult. Sanity comes into question, as does the lacklustre results of forced interaction with those who dwell on the other side of the Veil. Yet it need not be so. Opening yourself up to the presence of the spirit world is surprisingly simple, with the following techniques designed to offer a crash course in doing just that.

And I am speaking from experience here. After a particularly traumatic series of events in my teens I lost much of the natural ability to both see and hear beyond the material, though with the help of many years of retraining I have regained most of that initial skill and so much more besides.

While experienced practitioners may choose to skip over these steps in favour of their preferred methodology there is a lot of value to be gained from adding such lesser operations to your arsenal. A massively complex machine will only run efficiently if all the basic parts are in the right place, and that is doubly true for the esoteric arts.

Bone Glow Ritual

The first and most important technique that the adept can learn when just starting to work within this paradigm is to recognise their own bone glow. Unlike some of the other experiments designed to allow a steadily growing understanding of the unseen this core level task requires no tools nor lengthy rites to achieve noticeable results.

It also underpins much of the more advanced work within the necromantic sphere, as well as any related discipline which requires life force to function correctly too. Thus the operation lends itself to a variety of esoteric disciplines that demand a strongly defined sense of self. Which is almost all of them.

To begin the process the necromancer lays down in a quiet room and closes their eyes. It does not need to be dark, though subdued lighting may help with the next stage as once their breathing is calmed the attention is focussed beneath the skin and into the palm of their dominant hand. The fingers and thumb are then slowly flexed open and closed while the adept explores the bones inside with their mind's eye.

Visualising images of the underlying anatomy is unimportant at first, simply probing the tissues and tendons with directed attention will be enough. Once a feel for how everything fits together is gained, that point of interest is drawn back into the base of the wrist and then up the arm, joint by joint, before it is dragged over the shoulders too.

Focus is then moved down the other arm in a similarly methodical fashion before being held in the palm of the non dominant hand until dispelled through a sharp clench of the fist. As mastery of this first stage is gained the route of travel can then be fully visualised as an X-Ray image of sorts, glowing faintly against whatever is in the normal field of view with either open or closed eyes.

Anatomical correctness is not as important as an understanding of how those different internal mechanics feel when they interact, and just as with anything else the images which are seen by the mind's eye are not necessarily accurate in line with base reality. They represent the experiential side of being alive and are just as real as anything in a text book, while also carrying a lot of emotional weight as well.

Indeed, on repeated readings an astral armature of sorts can be developed, and if skilled with a pencil a fiercely personal image of that internalised structure cast to paper based on how the adept translates those scattered images into a human shape. A quick way to sigilise the self perhaps, though it is best to avoid sharing such internal descriptions with others just in case.

Of course this is just the simplest version of the operation, and as skill builds other parts of the necromancer's underlying physical structure can be explored via the spine and its skeletal offshoots before the ritual is concluded, perhaps hours later. This extends to muscle, cartilage and even internal organs, anything near to a bone is available to be experienced as a waking dream.

Directing that point of attention into the brain via the skull is very strange, but oddly comforting, as is the heart through the ribs. Blood flow can be followed, lungs felt cycling from full to empty and back again. Arthritis spiking and old breaks creaking. Aches and pains as swirling flowers in X-Ray negative. Ley lines of nerve endings telling secret stories of the world within. A life lived well etched under every inch of flesh.

The bone glow ritual is more than just an intriguing exercise in mind exploring matter, however. Aside from simply training both concentration and visualisation it also starts the adept down the path of energy recognition, an essential skill that underpins much of what they will eventually need to master while mapping the very boundaries of the seen and unseen worlds.

And once the necromancer becomes familiar with how their own body feels, glowing as it does against the concrete and brick of the mundane world, they will also become aware of the other points of light moving around them. Sometimes without an actual body at all, and this is where many that are just starting out along this cemetery path experience their first ghosts.

A quick bone glow can be undertaken almost anywhere. It is perfect for both magickal and mundane situations when the adept needs to feel grounded and braced against the swirling chaos around them. The operation is rarely dangerous to attempt as long as the adept is not in a situation where any form of altered state would be potentially hazardous anyway.

The ritual can also help them return to base reality after a particularly strenuous esoteric experiment, and allows for a mostly accurate monitoring of the bioelectric field if done regularly enough that potential issues are noticeable against the background hum of just being alive.

Death Stare Operation

Once upon a time I used to haunt old occult themed internet bulletin boards, soaking up as many of the copied and pasted excerpts being shared there as my painfully slow dial up would allow. Of course necromancy was always under-represented among my peers, so I learned to adapt other ide-

as to the task at hand instead.

As such what follows is my personal take on an often shared technique for building concentration, converted to a tool for forced clairvoyance by my very own hand. While still beginner friendly it has actually gone on to serve me well until the present day, and is especially useful when entering into unfamiliar surroundings for the first time.

Be they a witch, magickian or chaote, focus underpins much of the adept's training. Shutting out distractions and achieving such a narrow field of attention is mandatory for work with sigils, egregores and the successful deployment of most spells in general. Regardless of spiritual discipline one of the first things that needs to be learned is how to point the mind solely at a single objective.

Whether the adept actually ascribes any significance to the tools of their craft or just considers them props to help them get in the right mood, it is focus which adds the actual intent to the ritual being undertaken. Achieving the level of mastery required can be a difficult ask for those early in their esoteric journey. But there are very simple ways to get up to speed.

Of these, the most commonly described method to build inner will is to stare at a point in the distance while refusing to look away regardless of how much is going on around you. This can be done while walking towards that object or standing in one place, all that matters is that everything else is ignored.

Best conducted in familiar surroundings such as a bedroom or garden at first, it can be especially difficult for those who prioritise audio cues over visual. A good set of ear plugs can assist in the early stages of the training, though should not be used in busier locations or while in motion.

A variation on the above exercise involves the adept walking a relatively short distance to a point on a vertical surface, touching it and then turning around to walk back again, all the while focussing on a second but similar target in that direction. This is repeated until the movement and forced attention generate something bordering on a meditative state. And yes, this is a great way to fire sigils too.

For the necromancer, however, this laser like focus forms the foundation of the death stare operation, a ritual that is conducted to both gain a feel for the spirits in a certain location as well as allowing for brief glimpses of the history hanging in the air as well. It also points out areas of special energetic interest, such as particularly vibrant spikes of natural growth, though not always.

As with the basic process an object is initially chosen as a primary target for the adept's focus. As graveyards are a great place to train this enforced clairvoyance, a large or particularly striking memorial in the far distance is usually best, though in smaller rooms a mark on the wall or even eye level furniture can work.

The necromancer is looking to create a situation where their peripheral vision is actively enhanced, allowing them to see what is usually obscured by the more context rich information being received in their main field of view. And by overexerting their eyesight with intense focus before sharply releasing that pressure they are able to achieve such a starkly liminal state.

After staring for long enough to begin to block out everything but the point in the distance the adept relaxes and slightly crosses their eyes just enough to cause everything to lose definition while still maintaining a visual connection to the target object.

Anyone who has ever managed to make a magic eye picture work will recognise the methodology here. As the mundane visual echoes and ghostly lines caused by the retina continuing to feed old information through the optic nerve begin to die down, other images will briefly gather at the very edges of the necromancer's sight like moths dancing silently in negative.

As long as they are not stared at directly these new echoes will continue to ebb and flow. Some will be light, others dark, and a few may even be drawn to seemingly inconsequential objects, perhaps hinting at their significance. And if the location is spiritually active one or two could begin to move quite quickly, going about their business without realising that they have been spotted at all.

It is at this point that the necromancer may begin to experience clairvoyant flashes, jumbled or nonsensical as they may to be, a direct result of jump-starting their psychic faculties through the internal strain of stopping an otherwise enforced high level of focus dead in its tracks without the usual slow return to the mundane world.

As for winding up the ritual, the effects should wear off by themselves a minute or so after the vision is first relaxed. If a quicker end is preferred, perhaps due to the images being generated in the minds eye becoming distressing, then closing the eyes and rubbing them for a little while should suffice.

Despite this sharp shock to the system the death stare is generally safe to perform as long as the adept does not have a history of epilepsy or similar seizure generating conditions, and aside from the odd headache and a few minutes of eye strain when all is said and done the information that can be gained is worth the inconvenience.

Eternal Sleep Meditation

Perhaps it is a by-product of my neurodivergence, but I have never had much luck with the usual calming meditative techniques when done for their own sake. In general I do much better with excitatory stimuli such as overwhelming sound and quickly shifting images when forcing myself into the void.

Despite that personal quirk the following meditation does seem to work for me. While it is not one which I undertake regularly based on its locational requirements, especially as ghost hunting much less a factor in my life now, it has definitely served me well in the past.

Relying heavily on the skills nurtured through repeated experience with both the bone glow Ritual and Death Stare Operation, the following eternal sleep meditation is best performed in buildings that either have a haunted reputation or are suspected of being so.

As the name suggests the idea is to calm the mind enough to fall asleep, all the while remaining in a liminal state receptive to non-visual stimuli. This is achieved with little more than a king sized white sheet and a relatively comfortable bed, though a sleep journal is recommended to record the results as well.

To begin the necromancer lays on the first third of the sheet with their legs together and one hand by their side. The other is used to pull the remaining fabric over them and then tuck it underneath. This may take a little shuffling around to achieve the first few times, though the difficulty can be reduced significantly should the adept have someone willing to help at this early stage.

Once done correctly their head should be the only exposed area showing outside of the simulated burial shroud and their arms will have been returned by their sides, though not pinned in place. It is important that the mouth remains free from obstruction to mitigate the possibility of suffocation while sleeping, however. Nor should any knots be tied in the cloth in case of an overnight emergency either.

Once their eyes start to become heavy a full body bone glow is conducted, starting in the dominant hand before travelling all around the skeletal structure and any nearby organs before finishing in the other with the usual sharply clenched fist. By this point the adept should be almost drifting off to sleep, and the meditative phase of the process can begin.

The Death Stare is next, and while this is more difficult to do in a darkened room due to the lack of a focal point somewhere in the distance, the necromancer should still be able to see enough well even in low light to make out the ceiling or bunk bed slats above them in enough detail to allow for the process to work.

However it is less the energetic swirls that are the desired outcome here and more the usually fleeting images which sometimes accompany the operation when conducted in a more focussed and waking state. Indeed the adept actually refrains from breaking their focus in the usual way, instead allowing their vision to dim and eyes close as sleep overtakes them.

The desired liminal state at the core of the meditation is essentially enforced sleep paralysis. Recognised as a neurological aberration wherein either the dead themselves are easier to experience, or psychic impressions from the deep can mind flow unimpeded to the surface, the descent into slumber will be anything but normal.

Their resulting dreams should be vivid, potentially lucid and perhaps a little unnerving. While usually following some form of archetypal or even allegorical through line, they may well provide a window into the history of the location when dissected over breakfast the next morning.

Also in the moments before sleep overtakes the necromancer's already quietened mind the voices of the dead may become much easier to hear. While this interaction is admittedly one sided, leaving the adept with no choice but to listen to what they are told, it is still a useful way to confirm that the space is indeed active.

Vermin Totemics

Being an author I am blessed with the ability to see the world through starkly different eyes. Yet the narrative benefits of that remote viewing aside, such mental body doubling is a skill that has run like a vulpine thread through the weave of my esoteric life too. And all it took was the adoption of a totemic other, an internalised skin of autumnal red-brown fur to see me thrive.

As the name on this handbook suggests, the common European fox is my animal spirit of choice. Peerless interloper, these often misunderstood scavengers thrive in the shadow of the glass and concrete towers which rode like affluent glaciers over the underclass topsoil of my home town, destroying it utterly. But just like them I persist, evolving to feed on the scraps of culture those self important worthies left behind.

Necromancy is a discipline that relies heavily on the internal strength of the adept. Visualisation, intense concentration, void but receptive states and bioelectric manipulation. All these and more are required to face the shadows as an equal and not victim. But the revealing rays of sunlight can cause problems too, should the ignorant gaze of the uninitiated masses fall upon those walking along the cemetery path.

Of course, there are gods and goddesses who can help with the furtiveness required to avoid this potential conflict. Yet the less experienced adept may find value in taking onboard the guise of scavenger, furred and feathered invaders of the built human environment surviving despite the actions of those who would do them harm for just trying to find a meal. Strong, yet honest, medicine.

And so it falls to those creatures that crawl, skulk, skitter or glide to give the accelerated necromancer the power to view the world through the opportunist's lens. While there is value in forthright authenticity when walking beside the Reaper it is also worth recognising the need to keep the weirder side of an already strange life hidden from those who are unlikely to relish the presence of the death current in their world.

Badger

One of the more widespread mammals on this list, few outside of rural settlements will find any trace of the badger's passing. Yet these omnivores have been known to venture into town centres, scavenging rubbish piles or turned over bins to supplement their diet of insects, earthworms, grubs, young birds and hedgehogs. While some are solitary outside of mating season they have also been known to form larger clans too.

Dogs were once made to fight this noble creature for sport. Due to that and other martial associations these short legged members of the Mustelidae family are especially useful to the adept who is feeling embattled by the demands of those around them, both living and dead. Theirs are also the energies of grounding and rebirth, as can be seen with the folkloric role as sacred animal to the Celtic goddess Brigantia.

Brown Rat

Considered the filthiest and most dangerous of all the vermin listed here, the rat has a long and storied history of life alongside humanity. This cohabitation, while usually unwanted, stretches from the earliest settlements all the way to the modern era, and with the advent of sea travel also spread far across the globe. They form complex family groups, and seeing one usually means many more are nearby.

While their role in spreading the black plague is increasingly disputed they do carry other deadly pathogens, though domesticated breeds are generally safe. Of course, necromancers will have such a viral streak in their practice, a desire to spread their taboo ideas covertly within the cultural construct. And with a rich body of folklore tied to that exact idea any member of the Rattus family would be the perfect totemic choice.

Carrion Crow

The most recognisable of all the scavenging birds and one with a storied history in mythology and legend, the feathers of this highly intelligent and midnight black psycohpomp have long been prized in both ritual and dance. This is understandable, as accounts of them flocking to strip the flesh from the bones of the dead on ancient European battlefields has led to deep rooted chthonic associations that persist to this day.

While their need to socialise among their own kind differs between sub-species, the Corvidae family seems to share a common bond and will usually feed together on a corpse regardless. The absolute best choice as totem for both mediums and adepts that are often called upon to remove wayward spirits, their connection to the Morrigan allows for a level of command over the dead that few other animals share.

Coyote

An opportunistic pack hunter and eager scavenger, the coyote has had an easier time than most in working within the built environment that encroaches ever further towards their scrubland homes. Mistaken for smaller wolves by early European settlers within the Americas, their biology also ties them closely to the domestic dog. While they can breed with both of those related species the pup survival rate is low.

As with all members of the Caninae family these are are highly social animals, and therefore make fantastic totems for those who work within the necromantic field in cooperation with others. As such funeral directors, teachers and priests may benefit from this unruly yet gregarious medicine. From a folkloric point of view there is an entire corpus of tall tales revolving around this animal as trickster in First Nations lore.

Grey Squirrel

Interestingly, while the public perception of the squirrel is one of buried nuts and pilfered bird feeder seeds, they are in fact omnivores and will happily eat meat where available. As even the biggest specimens are still little larger than a rat, albeit sporting a much more impressive tail, they rely on scavenging during parts of the year where the usual insects, bird eggs and amphibians are unavailable.

A totem for those in the fields of communication and technology, these members of the *Sciuridae* family have a strong connection to weathering oncoming changes that may also be of use to the adept that finds their way to necromancy during a prolonged illness. As far as mythology goes, a special nod must be given to the occasionally foul mouthed *Ratatoskr* who carries messages up and down the Norse world tree.

Grizzly Bear

Less common within the built environment, bears tend to only be seen around border towns at the edge of their otherwise natural territory. This is slowly changing as human industrialisation continues to erode the forests and tundras which once supported them, though. Yes, some among their population have definitely started to see campers as an easy meal, but it is generally trail snacks and not the person that they are after.

The Ursidae family are mostly omnivores and will happily scavenge for whatever is available, aided by a fantastically acute sense of smell. The adept who prioritises a solitary walk along the cemetery path will find great value in this self sufficient energy, while those who are from a military background may also look to the rooted strength and savagery of the partially mythologised Viking berserker for inspiration too.

Red Fox

Recognised as seasoned interlopers into the urban sprawl, all breeds of fox are both highly adaptive with regards to habitat and also peerless scavengers when working within the city limits. Hated, hunted and used as trophies by the lords and ladies who claim dominion over the spaces that they once called home, these rebellious and sly shards of the nature current refuse to be brought low by rampant modernity.

The Vulpes genus of Caninae is a fantastic totem for the urban adept who must balance their esoteric pursuits with the types of mundane material concerns that force them to slink around secretly within polite society. Inari, the Japanese deity associated with rice, fertility and at one time even swordsmithing holds foxes as sacred, while tales of Reynard and his roguish travels were extremely popular in medieval Europe.

Seagull

Able to thrive in most climates and massively widespread across almost all continents of the world as a result, this once cliff based seabird has become a major urban scavenger in recent decades. Thriving on discarded kitchen waste or seen wheeling in large social groups over garbage dumps, these loud and in some cases physically imposing avians will readily attack people to snatch away their lunch if they can.

Yet when the main reason why they have been driven inland to survive is due to persistent overfishing and an ever diminishing aquatic food supply it is hard to think of them too harshly. Chosen of the Celtic sea god Manannan Mac Air, this is a dominantly resilient and cunning totem to adopt. As such the necromancer who needs to find a way to survive no matter the conflict that is causes should look to the Larus family for aid.

Raccoon

Dubbed the trash panda by city dwellers who witness the mess these nocturnal scavengers cause when rifling through their bins and dumpsters for scraps, the raccoon is an extremely intelligent animal who has ranged in small pockets far beyond its origins in North America. This spread is mostly due to failed attempts to promote them as pets, though considering the diseases they can carry ownership is generally a bad idea.

As the most famous of the Procyonidae family of omnivorous mammals they exude a deeply mocking rebellion and self centred aspect that would suit the less socially minded necromancer. They are also known to make their homes in abandoned structures, a quirk that might call to those who are forced to do the same through socioeconomic constraints. Like the coyote, they are seen as tricksters within First Nations tales.

Vulture

The vulture is by far the most obvious entry on any list of scavengers, though few realise just how often these large, once feared avians are sighted over the cities of the world. Clearing up roadkill and occupying a similar role as the seagull with regards garbage and waste piles, their stripping of carcasses to the bone is now thought to have historically prevented major outbreaks of disease and insect infestations too.

Seen as a bad omens or otherwise unclean due to their diet of dead flesh, both the New World Cathartidae and Old World Accipitridae families of large opportunistic carrion eaters share many traits while being largely un-related. Once tied to sky burials, they are a perfect choice of totem for the adept looking to embrace their inner ghoul, though this aspect can be an especially dangerous if handled incorrectly.

The Necromancer's Knapsack

While I would not necessarily bother with every day carry, there is a definite need for the accelerated necromancer to have easy access to the tools of their trade should something inexplicable occur. Yes, my auric skills are pretty formidable, and I rarely jump at all now. Which is a good start of course, but not everything can be so easily rebuffed by such self reliant means.

When going on an actual ghost hunt an inconspicuous method for bring along what amounts to an entire suite of esoteric technologies in as small a container as possible is a must. I personally use a simple black cross body bag with a couple of tactical pouches clipped on. So far at least this relatively simple solution has served me well with no eyebrows raised among my teammates on the night.

Yes, it really is a balancing act between having everything and the mortuary sink in one place while staying under the radar. More often than not this will be within unfamiliar locations among potentially uninitiated people of course. And unfortunately the minimum number of tools that the adept can safely get away with will only become clear with practice.

Tooth And Nail

While necromancers can hail from a number of different backgrounds, those who boast a more Neopagan origin will likely be well versed in the lore of herbs and stones. This is to be expected, for that well grounded, earthy denomination usually seek to utilise Gaia's bounty within their practice wherever possible.

And while this should never be overdone to the point that modernity is denied to prioritise some fictionalised version of the West's agrarian past, there is no harm in viewing the world through a hagstone lens. Even those who do not consider themselves to be witches will likely have a few candles lying around, and perhaps a crystal or two. All the batter to craft a welcoming and peaceful home.

At the opposite end of the spectrum are the classical adepts, high magick sorcerers that come from a background that prioritises circles of chalk, archangel names and religious admonitions to control spirits. These more formal necromancers may scoff at the importance of such physical objects, yet there is power in the treasures of the material realm. Especially when dealing with those who are no longer a part of it.

Despite the generally open handed style of sorcery that the more modern priests and priestesses of the Veil prefer, one which prioritises the aura, life force and willpower over wand and sword, there are still some general items that are worth keeping in reserve. And as for storing them until they are needed, a simple shoulder bag will do just fine. The more nondescript the better too.

That is not to say that it can be used without taking the time to properly consecrate it of course. All tools the necromancer adopts into their wider practice will inherently carry the energetic fingerprint of the people who created them. Indeed avoiding this additional contagion is why the adept should fashion as many of their ritual implements as possible themselves.

But larger items like knapsacks are too complex to hand stitch in most cases, and store bought are usually far less conspicuous out in the wild anyway. With this in mind a simple, and visibly hidden, empowering is undertaken to ensure that it feels right as a container for the far stranger things nestled inside.

On the bag is chosen, preferably one with a cloth lining that is separate from the rest of the outer skin, a small cut is made in one of the inside corners to gain access to the space at the bottom of the main compartment. The adept then deposits a few blunt coffin nails, some grave dirt and a handful of animal teeth into this void, before sewing it back together with a length of red thread. This need not be pretty, but it must be airtight.

The bag is then generously wafted with frankincense incense smoke by holding it open over the burning resin at a safe distance, and when enough has collected inside the flap is either clasped shut or zipped up to trap that sweet smelling smoke for a while. There is no need to do this every time the bag is opened, of course, just during the initial cleansing operation and only after the nails, dirt and teeth are buried in its folds.

Animal bones are also a viable option should teeth be unavailable, but these should be small enough to be hidden inside the lining of the knapsack without drawing undue attention or poking through to damage the contents. Same with the nails, blunt is preferred but not essential. The grave dirt is best taken from the resting place of a lawmaker, though any non-criminal batch will also generate the desired result.

The next consideration once the bag is ready is what to include and how to store it for travel. While general items such as rock salt or coffin nails should be in every necromancer's knapsack, there are a number of other items which have associations with the dead. And while there adept may have a natural affinity for the theatrical in their practice any tools should be safely stored and easy to access.

Dried herbs, salts and soil are best stored in corked or screw top test tubes as opposed to paper bags. This makes them easier to pour, and also keeps moisture damage at bay should the bag fall into a puddle or stream. Bones and nails are fine in drawstring pouches, but considering the risk of being scratched by the contents when rooting around in the knapsack looking for something these should be as thick as possible.

Liquids and oils work best in metal water bottles, though can be stored in plastic ones in a pinch. Finally any paperwork, such as maps or sigils that will be used repeatedly during a series of rituals or investigations are best kept within a notebook that is itself stored in a zip lock bag. This also a handy place to keep matches, batteries and a good sized orienteering compass as well.

The idea of trying to mitigate possible water damage may seem overly cautious at first, especially if lakes, pools, culverts or similarly aqueous places are not regularly encountered as the adept traverses their local landscape. But anyone who has ever been caught without a coat during a sharp spring downpour can attest that as little as ten minutes spent in a thunderstorm will ruin many months of hand written notes forever.

Organic Bounty

Even back when I was a more traditional Pagan there was no risk of me becoming a kitchen witch. I have never had much of a green thumb. And when the subject turns to herbs and spices my tastes are definitely on the hotter end of the spectrum. I can cook, sure, but I hate following recipes and prefer to wing it while reaching for a full jar of chilli powder. To be honest my approach to spellwork is much the same.

I do use certain botanicals in my wider necromantic practice though, and in various forms. So this admittedly short list of recurring tools has been built through many years of trial and error. It was never enough that someone mentioned a particular plant had associations with the death current. I needed to feel that connection for myself, and it is safe to sat that the results were not always what I expected.

Ease of access is an important consideration for the accelerated adept. While many of the necromantic operations outlined within the grimoire tradition call for strange and wondrous ingredients, this is not the case with the modern, death current based variation of the art. Simpler the better is the order of the day, as what the priest or priestess of the Veil does not need they also cannot lose.

No, the ability to freely acquire and then intelligently use the bounty of the natural world when working to help maintain the balance is a core tenet of this postmodern tradition, and a knowing nod to both the chaos magick meta-paradigm and Neopagan witchcraft traditions that heavily influenced its formation.

Familiarity with how a certain taste, smell or indwelling spirit will make the adept feel can only be gained through an actual working knowledge of that item. This, then, relies upon supply. As such, where a given ingredient is considered to be endangered or over farmed to the point that Gaia is actually harmed in its production then less damaging alternatives should definitely be sought.

Cinnamon

Despite its modern use within the spheres of both manifestation and healing magick, cinnamon also has a storied history with the dead. Especially wealthy Romans would have the aromatic bark added to their funeral pyres, while the Egyptians utilised it alongside Myrrh to help in the embalming process. A natural preservative, it is available in a variety of forms from powders to essential oils.

Larger cinnamon sticks are great for etching the names of departed loved one on before throwing the resulting talisman into the bonfire, a small scale re-enactment that calls back to those earlier funerary traditions. This will still carry power without the actual body needing to be close by. It can also be grated over apple scented candles before burning to further add an autumnal punch to the adept's ritual space.

Frankincense

Sold in a variety of forms this sweet but mellow scent is seen by many as the first choice for home cleansing and warding. Holding significance across the entire religious spectrum, at some point almost every denomination with historical connections to the Middle East will have used this pale blue smoke to mark out sacred spaces. Yet despite widespread use it is far from cost effective to obtain in its original resin form.

Of course there is a very real reason as to why this sticky brown sap is suddenly so expensive. Critically endangered due to the difficulty in cultivating new Boswellia trees while entire stands of them are also being cleared for agriculture, there is a definite risk that this most storied of winter aromas will soon be completely unavailable. As such the adept should strive to use only what little they need.

Garlic

A strong protective influence with an aroma so powerful that it literally crowds other scents out, both wild garlic and the more common cultivated bulbs can be used to add a punch to any cleansing or banishing. While some folklore actually ascribes both the origin of this plant and that of the onion to the footfalls of Satan after his fall, it is now especially prized as a ward against malicious spirits. And yes, vampires too.

Individual cloves crushed and swirled through warm water with some sea salt and dried sage work wonders as cleansing wash for the adept's other tools, and it can be broken up raw and rubbed into scratches or grazes that the necromancer receives while wandering through abandoned areas due to its natural antibacterial properties too. The leaves also dry pretty well, but lose a lot of their scent as they do so.

Oakmoss

Actually a type of lichen, this particularly pungent and woody symbiotic organism can be seen growing on oak, fir and pine trees. It has a number of pale green antler shaped fronds and even the relatively large clumps will only have a single anchor point attaching it to the bark. Due to that it is not uncommon to see the instantly aromatic ingredient scattered around the cemetery after a heavy storm, ready for collection.

Great to line offering bowls while it dries and then even better in home blended incense, the scent of this particular woodland staple has been described as somewhere between a damp forest clearing and sweet musk. As with all lichens it carries associations to do with renewal, rebirth and the interrelation of all things. When actually grown on oak it also shares that trees significance as a gateway to other realities too.

Pomegranate

Associated with Persephone's underworld imprisonment, the sharp and tangy nature of the deep crimson jewels held within the harder outer shell bring to mind late autumn and Samhain. Best used fresh, the juice expelled as the main body of the fruit is cut into can be used as a substitute for blood in sorcery and in this aspect harkens back to its supposed origins as a by-product of Adonis' death.

A natural antioxidant, those who find the idea of popping the individual seeds from inside tiresome can fall back on the wide variety of supplements and syrups available at most health food stores instead. The pure juice can be poured into cracks in rocky surfaces as part of an offering to the rulers of the underworld, while empty husks may be filled with herbs and buried beneath the soil for a similar effect.

Sage

Erroneously claimed as cultural appropriation in recent years, the history of using burning sage to promote harmony and protection in the living space actually goes back at least as far as the ancient Greeks. Smudging with shell and feather may be a tradition sensitive ritual, but the broader action of cleansing by smoke has little to do with a single ethnic group or geographic location.

While white sage is increasingly overharvested and may become critically endangered in the near future, the more common food safe garden variety shares many of the same clearing and warding properties while being easier to grow and more ethically sourced. For adepts who have issues when burning those smaller dried green leaves they can be crushed and used to dress candles or sprinkled over charcoal blocks instead.

Earthly Treasures

I have always been fascinated with minerals. When I was a child I would spend the majority of my dreary school visits to the Natural History Museum in London staring through the glass at the lustrous chunks carved from Gaia's rainbow hued bones, revelling in the hum that they sang in the cool climate controlled air. Like a magpie the twinkle called to me, and I found beauty in even the most caustic examples held there.

Of course the fact that I actively avoided the taxidermied animals in the upper galleries due to their hateful stares likely had a great deal to do with my growing elemental obsession as well. A happy accident, then, and a through line that would see me chase down books on the history of gemmology as readily as witchcraft once I began to take the idea of the occult more seriously in later years.

Gaia provides much to aid those who walk upon the cemetery path. As the broken wheel turns and Persephone begins the long journey to the underworld, her gaze will fall upon the richness that dwells beneath the surface. Each geode or cluster, vein or nugget a twinkling star within sunless caverns, illuminated by Hecate's brightly burning torches as she guides the young goddess down.

Rocks, stones, fossils. Metals and salts. Minerals of all shapes and kinds. As a discipline that belongs as much to the natural world as it does to the Veil, accelerated necromancers are adept at scavenging up the once precious treasures that can aid them in exploring both realms. And thankfully, at least where those who work with the dead are concerned, the costs to collect such trinkets remain relatively small too.

As with many forms of postmodern magick the adept is working with one eye to the past here, and another on synthesising those lessons towards a stable future where they can confidently hold their own. Mythology and folklore are not a solution in and of themselves. But there is a reason why so many witches and sorcerers fall back on those ancient stories in their esoteric practice. Whatever works, as they say.

Amethyst

Varying in hue from a pale lilac to a rich and deep purple, this relatively inexpensive variation of Quartz was once prized by nobility and has a long history of use by the wealthy. Amethyst scarabs have been found dating back at least to Egypt's Middle Kingdom, and etched Roman rings used the crystal as a canvas set within a golden mount. The Greeks famously used amulets of this mineral to prevent drunkenness too.

Once considered a cardinal gemstone, the discovery of large deposits in the Southern Hemisphere saw it downgraded relatively quickly, and this has allowed for a wider use. Adepts may be aware of the now completely discredited parts of its legend, such as an ability to rob poisons of their power. But one thing it can be relied on for is lessening the impact of recurring nightmares, an issue that many necromancers face.

Carnelian

A fiery orange to burning red semiprecious stone, this iron oxide infused chalcedony is best known for aiding in the control of anxiety by providing the courage to face deeply held fears. One of mankind's earliest mineral acquisitions, it has seen decorative use since at least the early Neolithic period and still maintains an unshakable fascination for many cultures from then through to today.

But there are necromantic uses too. Known in ancient Egypt as the blood of Isis, the Thet or Tyet amulet, often made of either carnelian or red jasper, would often be placed within the wrappings of the deceased, usually around the neck, to help ease the soul's journey through the underworld. This, then, is a handy tool for the adept looking to clear a path for loved ones as they reach their final hours.

Grave dirt

A staple of necromantic practice through the centuries, the earth from places of burial is widely recognised as a core ingredient for any number of esoteric recipes. Of course a respectful nod must be given to the hoodoo, conjure and root work traditions, as while these are not the origins of such after hours harvesting they have definitely cemented those practices within the wider esoteric community in recent years.

It is polite to ask the spirit who rests beneath the headstone if they will donate some of the soil from their resting place to aid in the success of the upcoming ritual. A coin flip can be used to capture the answer, and then left as payment if a yes is given. A no means moving on somewhere else. Care should be exercised when choosing a suitable grave, as the role that someone played in life will alter the overall associations.

Jet

A fossilised wood quite similar to coal, this unassuming mineraloid was created over many millions of years as ancient woodlands decomposed under extreme geologic pressure. It can be black or very dark brown, and will vary in hardness based on the salt content of the water that aided in its creation. A tendency to crack during more complex carvings aside, it sill lends itself to use in a variety of decorative objects.

As befits something so ancient the allure of the literal heavy weight of years held within will call to the necromancer, offering them the chance to interact with the concept of soil as a transformative catalyst. Those rituals undertaken using jet will allow for a small insight into what awaits the mortal shell after burial, as the semiprecious gemstone is itself the end result of such a subterranean evolution too.

Obsidian

Another mineral with a storied history, this cool, jagged volcanic glass has long been prized due to its ability to hold both a flawlessly polished surface as well as an unnervingly keen cutting edge. Lakes of crimson gore have been spilled by obsidian blades over the centuries, and while the Macuahuitle, or Aztec war club, is the most famous example other sharp weapons and tools were also regularly made of the material as well.

A naturally protective stone that is said to keep the adept safe from psychic assault, a suitably large and flat cut piece would work exceptionally well as a scrying mirror, allowing the necromancer to peer into other realms. If used to make a crystal ball then a sphere is cut instead. Care should be taken around untumbled examples, though, as it still hungers for blood and will happily take it from the careless adept.

Sea salt

A watery counterpoint to the more earthen minerals that seem to dominate the pagan space, salt is one of the few ritual ingredients that could be considered to be universally recognised across all esoteric paradigms. Once highly prized and taxed by the state, its use as a preservative allowed for wider travel and then trade between cultures in the ancient world. As such it remains intimately tied to human civilisation, even now.

It also has a definite spiritual element, perhaps because of its origins within the swirling oceans, and has long been said to protect from spirits, witches and the evil eye. Some necromancers will avoid adding salt to their altar in the belief that it will drive away the spirits they seek to attract, and while this is generally true it still remains the single best choice for drawing protective circles or warding sacred spaces.

Urban Spoils

Of course not everything that the necromancer uses in their practice will take such a raw, unprocessed form. I have personally acquired a number of intriguing tools over the last decade or so which are most definitely man made, and easily repurposed for my ritualistic needs. This was a pretty natural process, a slow accretion of magickal trinkets based on the spellwork being done at the time.

The following list is really just a guide as to what is out there in the built environment waiting for the crafty adept to stumble upon as they go about their day. Likely only a fraction of the potential materials to discover, what you choose to stock your knapsack with will of course be governed by both luck and personal taste. There are no wrong answers here, just varied individual needs.

Accelerated necromancers are perhaps a little more willing to incorporate man made items into their ritualistic practice than other traditions. Of course they are most often seen by the graveside, harvesting soil for whatever ritual needs arose on that specific day. And yes, crystals and herbs also make up a large part of their stored supplies too. But for more complex operations nothing beats repurposing mundane tools.

An ingenious species, humanity has sought to create change through invented objects since long before the industrial revolution began to bleed Gaia dry. And while many among the uninitiated would completely ignore the antique or outdated, blinded as they are by the onrushing wave of perpetual modernity, the history literally dripping from some of the following items will prove attractive to the inquisitive adept.

Not everything on this list is easily available, however. These are items better scavenged than purchased, though in some cases that may prove impossible. But if a fair price cannot be agreed then it is better to put those likely already limited funds towards other things, and trust that the tools will appear when the need is the greatest. Necromancy is a process, not at aesthetic, after all, and wisdom can never be bought.

Antique Surgical Tools

A favourite of those who collect macabre or otherwise eldritch items, the market for particularly fine examples of these once specialist implements with the associated provenience is strong even outside of esoteric circles. As such there are modern fakes on the market, though if purchasing in person the adept should be able to feel the history of the drills and blades upon even the most cursory of inspections.

It is rare to see these tools in a rusted state, seeing as they were mostly made from stainless steel, though the carry case is usually a little worse for the weight of years. Particularly well used sets will still hum quietly to themselves, reliving the flesh they have carved and lives which could not be saved. If the necromancer is looking for a wand to help focus their will there is no better item available second hand.

Black And White Photographs

While the majority of people have long since switched to digital options for storing their memories, up until the start of the 21st Century old fashioned film remained the medium of choice. As a result many homes still have a number of bulky and oddly discoloured photo albums in a cupboard somewhere, and derelict buildings always seem to have a couple of loose prints scattered around the place too.

Useful for sigil paper and when looking to invoke the memory of a certain person during a séance or dumb supper, bundles of these once universally cherished but now mostly devalued slips of thick paper and glossy chemicals can be seen for sale everywhere from charity shops to antique fairs. These are usually offered as materials for scrapbooking and as historical curios, or to fill out antique frames.

Coffin Nails

An obvious inclusion for those walking along the cemetery path, coffin nails come in a number of different shapes and sizes. Smaller iron tacks are relatively common, though much wider, flat headed examples can be found in the wild as well. This is a rare example of something harvested from burial plots by the adept which will not offend the balance, as long as the coffin is already exposed to the elements.

Care should be taken when extracting them though, as they are usually rusty and perhaps quite jaggedly sharp too. A pair of pliers may be the best way to go, and a thicker grade of draw string bag used to carry them home. For those who do not have access to the required gardens of the dead, a number of online speciality stores usually have bags of them in stock. This can provide a safer, if more expensive, solution.

Mourning Jewellery

Mostly hailing from the end of the 19th Century, the latter years of the Victorian Era in the United Kingdom has long been seen as a major waxing of the death current within that cultural landscape. The queen lamented the loss of her husband to such a degree that she retreated from society, and in doing so drew the easily impressionable members of the upper and middle classes into a vast, ritualised nationwide sorrow.

Thus keepsakes and trinkets became the order of things. Back jet and shiny onyx with gold and silver trim. Lockets, chains, broaches and pins. The hair of the deceased or, depending upon the year, perhaps a photo instead. These items tend to have a sad charm to them, especially when the family line described has long since died out, and while costly are perfect for adding a definite necromantic hum to modern clothes.

Out Of Date Maps

There is power in understanding the evolution of the city, especially where those points of interest intersect with the resting places of the dead. Not only does this allow for a better grasp of the history of thin places such as cemeteries and hospitals, but may also provide an insight as to why more modern buildings smell so strongly of death without any obvious reason. Necrogeographic waypoints in the making for sure.

Many locations are plagued with the memories of what was once on the land centuries before, or even just the atrocities which occurred there. A collection of such documents moving as far back in time as is easily available can also help trace the original boundaries for when the adept desires to meet with the spirt of place through ritualistic means. The city centre is rarely the historic core of the urban sprawl, after all.

Second Hand Mirrors

Slightly harder to find due to the public perception that such things are worthless, old mirrors are a must have for the necromancer who wishes to improve upon their scrying ability and psychic visions. These need not be painted black to work, as the only requirement to attune them to the death current is that they were originally used in either a retirement home, hospital or asylum for any number of years.

This may seem a needlessly sour tool to the more love and light focussed practitioner, but a mirror that is pre-encoded with sorrow is perfect for divination while inside supposedly haunted locations. If a broken example is found then the edges are only safe if taped, and it is best to keep the entire surface wrapped in black cloth when not in use just in case something decides to use it a doorway instead.

Silver Sixpences

A folkloric staple in stories revolving around ghosts and their removal, this particular coin was even said to have been loaded into flintlock pistols to keep the dead at bay when rakish nobles would find themselves dared to stay overnight in dangerously haunted locations. They are now abundantly available from most dealers, though a certain amount of care should be used to check the date when purchasing.

Sterling silver was only the main ingredient in examples minted until 1920, while those up to 1947 are a fifty fifty blend with other metals. Any dated between then and 1980, when the coin was retired as legal tender, will be a copper and nickel alloy instead with no silver included in the mix at all. The oldest variants can be very expensive, but are worth the investment if the adept is looking for small but effective amulets.

Bulk Animal Bones

A slightly quicker method to acquire animal skulls and teeth for ritual purposes, these once living objects are usually sourced through listings on-line. They tend to be a poor substitute for remains recovered by the adept in the wild, but depending on the amount of green space available in the local landscape the choice may need to be made to fall back on store bought. And when nothing else is available there is no real reason not to.

Junk and curio shops usually have a few examples of taxidermy on display, though these do not always include the fully posed anatomy beneath and as a result are better left for people who wish to keep them as art objects instead. Specificity articulated skeletons can be broken down into their constituent pieces, though again this is far from cost effective. Individually sold bones are usually the best value for money overall.

Crafty Crafts

The general level of mistrust for those who claim to walk the cemetery path necessitates that they take the time to create much of their own equipment. Indeed, in the last twenty or so years I have found very few occult supply stores that carry the kinds of ingredients that I need straight off the shelf. Not that this is an issue, especially as the act of invention adds to the overall power of those tools anyway.

Many a weekend I have walked the lesser travelled boundaries of my local graveyards, cloth bag in hand, harvesting what I need right under the nose of those who were there for far more acceptable reasons. Seeing as my general ethos is to leave the remains of the dead well enough alone there has yet to be any issue with my taking a handful of animal bones or the odd fragment of marble instead.

Of course every aspiring priest or priestess of the Veil will gravitate towards the death current in slightly different ways, and ever the creative I have found a number of useful resources that lend themselves to doing just that. Whether it is attracting, repelling or harnessing the powers of the dead, there is much to be gained by getting your hands just a little dirty.

Harvesting Ingredients

As a path that pays special attention to the actions of scavengers within the urban landscape, it is no surprise that much of the accelerated necromancer's arsenal would be created from found materials. Many of the following handmade tools rely heavily on the very items that most who drift between the gravestones would never notice, remaining safe to collect with little chance of repercussion as a result.

And by far the easiest of these ersatz items to find is grave glass. Usually seen as jagged bottle green chips on flatter burial plots, both clear and blue variants remain relatively common depending upon both location and supply. Marble chipping is also used for this purpose in some areas, though has no real value to the adept and is best left alone.

While an amorphous substance and not a true crystal, the unordered nature of its molecules has led many adepts to treat glass as a poor substitute for more mainstream materials such as quartz or selenite. Yet to dismiss this mostly man made object is to also ignore one of the best death current batteries outside of coffin nails and grave dirt.

Far easier to find than those more popular ingredients, it can be harvested right under the noses of the general public with a little slight of hand as well. It is easy to underestimate just how much energy those seemingly mundane little fragments will soak up over time.

As such while an earlier date on the burial plot of choice is no guarantee of the age of the associated glass, the skilled necromancer will definitely be able to tell which ones are ready to harvest with a simple wave of their hand. It has been described as a cool warmth, something like ever building frostbite, and an electric tingle will announce the presence of a particularly vintage batch.

Grave glass is a little awkward to use however, and could be considered dangerous in the unlikely event that it was even possible to grind the shards down into powder, so any tools should exclusively use the ingredient in its whole, chipped form as found.

While there is little danger in tumbling them to smooth out the sharper edges it is also unlikely that any residual cemetery essence would survive the process, and as a result may only be relevant for aesthetic and not practical purposes in similar ways to which old bottle glass can be used.

Bones are next, though not those of human origin. As stated elsewhere, the seven necromantic laws forbid the modern necromancer from interfering with bodily remains, even when the heat cracked soil itself offers up such things to the waiting sky.

If anything the adept should just say a soft prayer of safe journey to the spirit which once inhabited those jumbled remnants and then move on to search elsewhere, once a few of the more easily accessible coffin nails are saved for later. To the living the spoils, as they say.

Animal bones are fair game, however, and it is not uncommon to find a heap of bird skulls or random ribs and wing bones too. Any associated feathers can also be useful, and indeed a pile of such now grounded plumage may be present when the remains themselves have been dragged away by whatever decided that pigeon or sparrow was on the menu.

Water can be collected from divots in the outer body of flatter grave markers, though due to the chance of contamination or lack of availability during the hotter summer months it may be preferable to leave a jar of spring water somewhere inconspicuous and pick this up once it has been given the chance to charge, preferably new moon to new moon.

Potions created in this manner are not for human consumption and should be considered external use only. Regardless of intention liquid that has pooled within the interior of an exposed burial should be avoided due to the dangers associated with the decompositional processes which may still be taking place.

While alcohol can also be left to the elements in a similar way, this works better as an offering to the inhabitants of the graveyard itself and will rarely pick up much of a charge due to its already fiery aspect. Trees which sit within the boundaries of a burial plot also offer possibilities to the crafty adept, and the broken dryads among them will happily take a swift drink if the opportunity arises.

Growing as they do with roots laid down inside the surrounding graves, both life and death are represented within their whispering trunks. Soil dug from around the roots of such a liminal interloper has a uniquely entropic essence that lends itself to healing operations, while fallen slabs of corpse gorged bark make great offering dishes on the necromancer's altar, though will eventually crumble over time.

The sawdust from a recently felled tree can make a fantastic core for home blended incense once allowed to dry for a month or two, and the same can be said for freshly cut branches, though these are best used to make ash through adding them to a ritual fire outside. Fallen twigs after a particularly heavy storm can also work well in similar circumstances.

Nuts, seeds and berries are a perfect addition to seasonal bowls dotted around the magickal laboratory, as well as in regular herbal blends. Mosses from the surfaces of grave markers can be brought home and dried, as long as no damage is done to the memorial by doing so, but care must be taken when burning these due to the potentially acrid smoke which can result.

Finally, while it is rare to see fruit trees within a cemetery, the produce that grows there is generally safe to consume. It can work as a substitute of sorts for the human flesh in more traditional necromantic rituals, though few which call for that macabre ingredient are of any real value. Much like the jars of water mentioned previously this is at the adept's own risk, of course, though is preferable to the alternative.

Foxfire Salts 2.0

An updated and empowered version of my ground-breaking foxfire salts blend, this uniquely adaptable tool has served me well in a variety of ritualistic situations over the years. I have drawn many a boundary with this chalky powder, including when sealing a panic room or two, and I always keep a vial in my knapsack for those just in case scenarios that may occur at a moments notice.

As the name would suggest, foxfire is both more fiery and adaptable than the list of supposedly mundane ingredients would initially seem, and it becomes potent beyond measure when fermented for a month or more beneath the earth. Best to keep the liquid version away from plants and soft furnishings though, as it will definitely stain. The smell is also beyond terrible too, though I think that adds to the charm.

Ingredients

Allspice powder
Chalk dust
Garlic powder
Grave dirt
Sea salt
Iron filings

Optional

Chilli powder
Coffin nails
Grave glass
Tomb wash
Olive Oil
Rust flakes
Sulphur

Tools

A glass or earthenware jar with lid

Foxfire is an easy blend to create, with the only real issue resulting from balancing the overall ratio of ingredients when some of the optional items are added to the mix. As a rule of thumb it works best when all the parts are measured equally, except for the olive oil or tomb wash which are combined with the dry blend until the desired consistency or dilution is achieved.

Starting with the grave dirt and chalk dust in the base of the jar, stir in the garlic and allspice powders before adding the courser sea salt and iron filings, the latter of which is available online should local suppliers be difficult to find. Screw the lid and shake gently while focussing on your intent. The following ritual chant may assist with imprinting this on the foxfire as it churns away in the container.

"Garlic and allspice grown in the grave dirt.

Iron and chalk below the salted sea.

All six charms I call to my defence.

I draw these marks and spirits heed."

The lid is then gifted a single drop of the necromancer's own blood before being sunk beneath the earth for a lunar month, new moon to new moon. A general prayer to the gods or goddesses of choice can be intoned at this stage, though the above chant will also work just as well for those adepts who have yet to foster a relationship with the spirits who oversee the integrity of the Veil.

This mock burial need not be conducted within the bounds of a cemetery to work, and is equally effective when done in a garden or woodland clearing away from judgmental eyes. Allspice powder is often used in healing blends, and promotes both vitality and virility. Neither are things which the dead are known for, so lends itself as a repellent in line with the rest of the blend.

Garlic is naturally protective and banishes the supernatural, while sea salt has a similar history among European cunning folk. This passive warding aspect is shared by iron, though it also has a martial tang through its association with Mars, and using the metal as filings ensures that the pointed ends will be aimed at the incoming threat.

Grave dirt adds both earth energy and works as a conduit for the death current, while chalk is simply a neutral carrier medium designed to aid the flow of the overall mix when poured. When expanding foxfire for a specific purpose the core ingredients should be left unaltered.

That said, rust flakes, coffin nails and sulphur can be added to boost the repellent power of the blend when dealing with particularly persistent ghost-forms or echoes, though as with the other large ingredients this will effect how well it pours when drawing circles on the ground or altar space.

Chilli powder increases the firey nature of the otherwise cold necromantic mix and works well in hexing operations against the living. Grave glass is attractive to ghosts, pulling them close to be rebuffed by the rest of the mix. Olive oil and tomb wash will altar the overall consistency based on ritual specific needs, and can add their own minor associations as well.

Grave Glass Cookies

While the usefulness of passive spell effects within a given location is often overlooked, there is a great deal of power in marking the space out as sacred to the Veil. Best seen as small, single purpose beacons of the necromancer's will designed to either repel or attract the wandering dead, I personally swear by these in both my home location and when setting up a panic room should a ghost hunt go sour.

Like any tool which relies upon stored cemetery essence to function they will not run indefinitely, so I often find myself making a new batch around Halloween. Considering that this usually coincides with a dedicated autumn effort to harvest some of the other ingredients used in my workings it can be guaranteed that these highly inedible cookies will boast the longest possible shelf life before needing to be replaced.

Ingredients

Air drying clay
Grave glass

Optional

Amethyst
Animal bones or teeth
Coffin nails
Bloodstone
Obsidian
Smoky quartz

Tools

Greaseproof paper

The colour of air drying clay used in the construction of these tools is generally unimportant, though it can be chosen specifically to tap into the wavelengths associated with the desired effect. Black is a good general purpose choice, and undyed clay works well too though is less visually appealing. This can be of use should the necromancer need the cookies to blend in with the background in an otherwise public place.

Once the clay is chosen it is cut into as many equal sized chunks as desired and each is flattened against the palm of the left hand to create an obvious circular biscuit shape around an inch thick at the edges and a little more towards the centre. This is so it does not fall apart when the other ingredients are pushed through the surface, and the air drying variety is deliberately chosen so that nothing need be put in the oven to harden.

Grave glass cookies come in two distinct flavours. For the repelling version, designed to ward a space from unwanted spirits, the central focus is either bloodstone or obsidian. This is socketed into the middle of the disk, facing upward. Coffin nails are next, five to be exact.

These are pushed through the base of the disk and at a slightly outward facing angle away from the core stone. Finally five good sized shards of grave glass are pressed down into the outer third of the clay, again angled slightly away from the central point.

Bloodstone is used to bolster courage and banish negativity, similar to obsidian which also protects from emotional harm. Coffin nails have a duel role as attractors of wondering spirits as well as a barrier to their passing by virtue of the sanctified burial they represent. Finally grave glass, while intriguing to the dead, also sets the background hum for the whole endeavour here.

Attracting cookies are created in a similar way, though either amethyst or smoky quartz is used for the core stone. Both of these promote healing and open the third eye for psychic work, with the latter also generating emotional calm for both the living and the dead as well.

Bone is a reminder of physicality. This is something that many spirits, be they classical wondering souls or the more accelerated ghostforms yearn to recapture, and can be substituted for animal teeth if they are readily available. Either way, this type of item is a fantastic addition to the adept's workspace, and can be left pulsing away on their ancestor altar for many months until running out of steam.

Crown Of Thorns

It is a fact of life that adepts who spend any real time around haunted houses or graveyards run the risk of something unwanted following them home. Yes, necromancers are uniquely suited to banishing operations, yet it is far easier to ward your location ahead of time and not have to bother.

Interestingly, the crown of thorns can be used as a mobile magick circle if enough ribbon is used to create a comfortable space inside, though I find that this only works if the majority of nails face the outside of the curve. I have also worn it looped through my belt when sitting vigil in a haunted location, though this may have been overly cautious as nothing really happened all night.

Ingredients

Black ribbon
Iron nails
Grave glass
Tomb wash
Foxfire salts

Optional

Coffin nails
Green ribbon
Red ribbon

Tools

A glass or earthenware jar with lid

The trickiest thing about creating a crown of thorns is the tying of the multiple knots. These are open for personal interpretation, as long as they allow for the insertion of the iron nails or slivers of grave glass just before being pulled tight. As such one with a natural looping effect is recommended though not mandatory.

Once the desired length is chosen two strands of ribbon are lined up closely parallel with each other and a first knot tied about a third of the way down their length. This not only connects the two strips together but also creates enough space to attach the crown of thorns to something at the desired location.

As each subsequent knot is made but before it is fully tightened a nail or grave glass piece is inserted in the loop. The following banishing call is a strong option to help imprint a protective intent in the otherwise mundane ingredients while the resulting node is being pulled closed.

"Ribbon veins and rusty Nails.

Deny the advance and bleed the soul.

Knots a puzzle which cannot be solved.

Off you go to seek easier prey."

Once this is complete the adept moves on to the next one, tying each around an inch below the last so as to allow for some flexibility once the crown is complete. This sequence continues down to the bottom of the ribbon, which is finally tied off in a similar way to the top so as to not unravel over time. It is then carefully dipped into a container of tomb wash and allowed to drip dry outside overnight.

Should the large circular version be preferred the creation process remains largely the same, though the top and bottom are tied together at the end of the operation to form a continuous sequence of nails and grave glass to the desired radius. The natural shortening in length during the knotting process should also be considered, and more ribbon than initially planned allowed.

As stated before, Iron is both warding and martial in nature due to its associations with Mars, while grave glass creates a cold hum of the death current along the knotted strands. Tomb wash further bolsters the otherworldly polarity of the crown as it soaks into the very fabric while adding its own ingredients and their associations to the mix as well.

Both green and red ribbon can be combined with the black to add to the overall aesthetics of the crown, and coffin nails mixed in with the iron ones should enough of a supply be held within the necromancer's knapsack to allow for this.

Smaller crowns can be hung around the entrances to the adept's home or magickal laboratory, while the circular ones make fantastic portable ritual circles for panic room scenarios or other non permanent ritual sites. They do tend to be difficult to conceal when in use, however, and care should be taken handling the sharper edges during transit.

Tomb Wash

A fantasticality versatile base medium for any number of necromantic liquids, a quick jar of tomb wash can be made with very little preparation. Empowered by the marble of the grave markers themselves it can be used almost straight away without charging, though there is an empowered variation which requires just that and offers a little extra kick for the added effort.

I tend to use this in the liquid version of foxfire salts, or to cleanse new implements and tools before adding them to either my altar or knapsack. Best not to try to drink it though. The creation process necessitates that the once pure water comes into contact with some less than hygienic surfaces, so renders it strictly for external use only.

Ingredients

Bottled spring water
Sea salt

Optional

Frankincense resin

Grave glass
Grave marker fragments
Human teeth
Silver sixpences
Smoky quartz
The adept's blood
The adept's hair

Tools

A glass or earthenware jar with lid
Black ribbon

While the actual mechanics of creating a jar of tomb wash are simple, the preparation beforehand will differ depending on the eventual result. That said, all that is required for the base blend is a store bought bottle of spring water, a handful of course sea salt, a jar of some kind and a suitable tomb.

Then the adept has only to pour the liquid onto the inclined surface of a grave marker, letting it travel as it may both across and down the marble, before catching as much of the run off as possible in the jar. This is then sealed with black ribbon until needed, and while only using two ingredients is perfectly serviceable for less complex applications such as the cleaning of ritual tools before use.

The intermediate blend is infused with grave glass fragments, a handful of course sea salt and a single inch or so sized fragment of headstone or grave marker, freely found and not chipped off by the necromancer themselves. These solid ingredients are placed in the jar ahead of time and become submerged once the water is added through the usual pour and capture process.

A stronger version can be created by hiding the water in the cemetery for a lunar month, new moon to new moon, to soak up even more of the surrounding energy before it is added to the mix. This is not usually necessary, but if the liquid from the jar is to be further diluted by straining and adding to a floor wash used in clearing an entire living space, then is actually recommended so as to keep the general necromantic hum.

For dire situations, such as the countering of hexes, a far more complex mix of ingredients is needed. The adept places offcuts of hair and a few drops of their blood into the jar along with a tooth if one is freely available, such as after recent dental work. Sea salt is mandatory too, of course.

Grave glass and a small fragment of shipped headstone are laid on top before silver sixpences, frankincense resin and smoky quartz are carefully stirred in too. The jar will likely be quite full at this point, but there should be enough room to pour the lunar month charged water in as well, via a tomb as usual.

This witch bottle in all but name will absorb the incoming negativity when placed on a windowsill near where the adept sleeps, smelling as it does of both them and death as well. If used during a prolonged run of bad luck this may even prove a strong enough pull on whatever is dogging the necromancer's steps to draw it away. While not a permanent solution, it will grant enough of a respite to ground and rebalance.

Frankincense resin has a long history of use in religious rituals and offers the adept both a purifying and calming influence. Grave glass is of course the conduit of the death current that powers the jar, while the grave marker fragments offer a low hum all of their own to the mix. Smoky quartz is a healing and psychically active stone, levelling out the otherwise disharmonious energies used elsewhere in the jar.

Silver sixpences have long been considered to be an effective ward against evil, though only ones minted up until 1920 are actually made almost exclusively of that material. Later coins up to 1947 are a fifty fifty blend, while any dated between then and the retirement of the coin in 1980 will exclusively be a copper and nickel alloy instead. As such earlier examples are far more useful in magickal work than the latter.

The adept's blood, hair and teeth are designed to create a decoy that smells like them in times of need, and the black ribbon is really just for ease of storage as once this is removed the necromancer should recognise the batch as used, regardless of how much remains.

Tomb wash is initially quite a strong necromantic blend, but it does run out of bite over time. All individual ingredients aside from the sixpences and quartz are to be discarded once the tomb wash has been used for something, even if the whole jar is not completely drained, and the blended liquid poured into a fast running stream, preferably under the cover of darkness where prying eyes will not witness the deed.

The Wraith Jar

There is a long tradition in English folklore of praying ghosts into bottles, before throwing them into lakes or wells never to be seen again. While the religious overtones of this procedure leave me cold, I have experimented with the idea of trapping the dead and then moving the resulting problem elsewhere. This capture and release is more of a passive process though, as the unseen world rarely does as its told.

Plus when the only thing actually stopping the ghostform or echo from exiting the trap is the quality of the bait the real issue is speed of delivery. This eventual destination can either be a cemetery or someone else's home based solely upon the necromancer's mood, and both are equally valid depending upon the actual situation at the time. As long as the balance is served there is no need to worry about moral judgements.

Ingredients

Animal bones or teeth
Coffin nails
Grave glass
Grave dirt
Olive oil
Tomb wash
Wax

Optional

The Adept's blood
The adept's hair

Tools

A glass or earthenware jar with lid

The wraith jar is not a trap in the classical sense. There are no runic wards or lengthy incantations designed to work like astral flypaper, nor is the entity really confined within the vessel outside of their desire to feed holding them in place. It instead capitalises upon the hunger and single minded nature of most ghostforms or echoes, using their own greed against them while the reserves of graveyard essence within are drained.

The dry ingredients are added to the container first, with the grave glass and coffin nails as the first layer, then animal bones or teeth for the next. A few capfuls of olive oil are poured over this mix of jagged shards to simulate the slurry that collects within older graves, before the wax is poured heavily over the top, burying the rest of the ingredients. Ideally this should be at least a few centimetres thick all round.

Tomb wash is then mixed with grave dirt until the resulting fluid is at least cloudy if not almost syrupy, and then pored into the remaining space within the jar. This should only be done once everything else has cooled and set so as to prevent the liquid making contact with the olive oil. The lid is then put on and the newly created ritual object is placed in a shadowy part of the living space, away from pets or children.

As the grave dirt settles to the wax over the next week, so too will the hungry astral entities within the building be drawn to the nails and bone burred beneath. Once the sedimentation has completed only clear water should be sitting on top. At this point the entire object is moved to another location, be it a dilapidated cemetery or someone else's living space.

The partitioning of the dry ingredients in the jar is designed to create a mock burial of sorts. Both the grave glass and animal bones will carry the death current's unique essence, attracting anything looking for an easy meal. The coffin nails further represent this idea, while the olive oil sloshes around the base of the container coating the other items and preventing their energetic signature from evaporating too quickly.

The wax is purely a barrier between the two sets of fluids, and while black would be preferred brown also lends itself to the illusion that a slice of the graveyard has been uprooted and added to the jar like a packed lunch for the wondering pseudo-entities which plague the home, a transformation of base ingredients into unnatural diorama that is at the core of what the necromancer is hoping to achieve.

Finally, should the initial attempts at creating a wraith jar fail to attract anything, slightly more drastic action can be taken. In this case actual life force is added to the dry ingredients before the olive oil is poured. The necromancer can use their own blood and hair or that of someone in the afflicted home, though as with all operations the balance must be respected and such ingredients should be only taken with permission.

Once the ritual concludes and the resulting jar has been disposed of, the living space should be subjected to a full cleanse to deter any further infestations from occurring. This is never completely effective though, so perhaps the opportunity should be taken to see if anyone living there has the untapped psychic potential that both attracts astral parasites and also makes them a possible candidate for the cemetery path as well.

Ground Rules

I have been ghost hunting off and on since my teens. Starting solo with ill advised midnight sojourns into the derelict periphery of London's urban regeneration, the constant tug of war with security guards and damaged flooring soon led to my membership of a handful of semi-professional teams both there and in my current city too.

Here I stayed only as long as it took to learn the tricks of the trade, and to be honest the lack of intellectual rigour and delusional thinking on display in most of them was enough to put me off the idea of group work for many years after. The sticky smell of Spiritualism, itself mired in Christian heresy and mistrust of the very same dead which they hoped to make contact with, also made me seek the door as fast as possible.

But there were some good aspects to my time stalking through many of those same buildings from my urban exploring days, just post renovation and with the owners paid permission. I may have been keeping my necromantic interests under a general veneer of bland pseudoscientific inquiry, but throughout the night my mind was ever on darker things.

The P7 Protocol

The prevailing feeling among the uninitiated majority is that ghost hunting is a dangerous and potentially soul destroying hobby. While the necromancer will naturally gravitate to the dark places that others instead avoid, the accusation that paranormal investigation of any type should be approached with all due precautions is not an untrue one.

Adepts from any Veil adjacent discipline will be well versed in the arts which allow then to work safely in haunted locations without the risk of entities following them home. And if they do, a decisive action to cleanse and ward the living space is usually enough to see them off again with the minimum of fuss. For everything else on the night, there is the P7 protocol.

By far the biggest potential risks are planted firmly in the material realm, and involve the various ways in which the living or location can make it a night better left unremembered. That is not to say that the dead are never an issue as well, of course, just not one as immediately threatening as the fabric of the building and the adept's companions during a particularly chaotic vigil.

One: Preparation Is Key

By far the most obvious entry on this list, the first thing that the accelerated necromancer should check is that they have all the relevant equipment sorted and available. They will also need a viable way to carry those implements to the location, a knapsack being the easiest method. A fresh batch of foxfire in a corked test tube and small crown of thorns on the belt are a must, while some sea salt may also be needed.

If others who do not know about the adept's more taboo interests then those esoteric implements should be very well hidden under the expected voice recorders, torches, tape measures and perhaps a multi tool if the location is especially derelict. Spare batteries and a waterproof notebook are worth taking as well. Chalk can also prove useful for marking potentially mobile objects, though should be erased at the end of the night.

Two: Physical Health Matters

More so than even the most naive of the uninitiated, the necromancer must be confident in themselves before embarking on an investigation, especially those where strangers will be present. Creating a bland cover story to avoid pointless deviations into sceptic versus believer territory aside, there is also the ever present issue of smelling like the Veil to anything in the location that would be drawn to such things as well.

The adept's current health therefore becomes important. While the worst is unlikely to happen, making either a panic room or quick and dirty banishing necessary, any illness would render their most important diagnostic tool unreliable. It is almost impossible to read a room when every joint aches from the flu, after all. In those cases cancellation and long stint under a blanket would be the best outcome for all concerned.

Three: Permission Must Be Sought

While the dead rarely pay much heed to boundaries the living must play by such earthly rules. As a result the necromancer and their allies should always try to seek permission from the landowner unless the building is long abandoned. There is little reason to visit semi-derelict locations alone when the area is particularly full of them, as local ghost hunting groups will likely be running fully insured events there eventually anyway.

Even then, when security or police interference is not an issue, other risks present themselves. If the adept regularly works with candle flames during the divinatory phase of an on site investigation then the building managers may have rules against their use for health and safety reasons. Same goes for incense or salt circles too. Plus such empty structures are a haven for crime or, more worryingly, the stashing of dead bodies.

Four: Precautions Are Put In Place

It is important that the necromancer get know the location ahead of time, especially if it is mostly derelict. Exposed piping, missing stairs, even something as mundane as a partially bolted handrail can quickly end a night in tears. And the problems are not always immediate either. Asbestos fibres for example, or respiratory disease causing moulds minding their own business in the dark, waiting to ruin the maskless visitor's life.

Understanding how the floor plan matches up to the real world state of the building really does become a matter of life and death when the especially unprepared take one step too far and wind up making a high speed descent down the nearest lift shaft. Without the lift, of course, and possibly among friends. Perhaps this scant regard for personal safety is to be expected of hobbyists, but the adept must set a better example.

Five: Personalities Are Always A Factor

While the necromancer should try to avoid investigating alone for safety reasons, they should also choose their companions well. Psychic ability is no compensation for an irrational fear of the dark, nor does access to a usually barred location make up for that person also displaying stress related anger issues. Past trauma is a given in the fringe which the adept inhabits, but can become an explosive problem if triggered.

In paid for public events the adept will of course have no say in how this mix is created. Such a loss of control can be circumvented by calling on a few trusted friends to come along for the evening ahead of time. If no one is available then a quick read of the room should highlight those in the crowd with the most experience, as well as people best avoided and left to their potentially dark fate when the lights go out.

Six: Professionalism Above All Else

Necromancers do best in the shadows. There is nothing to be gained from exposing the working of the Veil to the uninitiated, nor would the more pseudoscientific among the membership be best pleased about having what they perceive as a credulous fool within the ranks of their paranormal investigation group either. In such cases it is best to defer to the methods of the organisation, at least on the surface.

It is only polite for the adept to carry out the roles which they have been assigned, be it note taker or silent watcher, and this will maintain a plausible cover while they instead use their more mediumistic abilities to probe the atmosphere around them. Death stare operations can be completed in silence, requiring very little movement, while Ouija and seances are enhanced simply through the adept's involvement.

Seven: Postgame Checklists

For the necromancer, unlike the other investigators in attendance, the night does not end with the first rays of dawn. Once they have returned home all of the ritual tools which they took with them must be cleansed to prevent bleed through from the location just visited, and any foxfire poured replaced from the adept's main supply. Mundane items like voice recorders or torches can also be recharged at this time too.

Once they have showered or bathed to help realign their bioelectric field it is advisable to perform a full bone glow ritual to make sure all is as it should be on a physical level. A quick check around the living space and the wards which keep it free of wandering entities is next. Then and only then is the hunt truly over, and they can start to look through the audio and video evidence that they collected along the way.

What The Dead Are Attracted To

It always surprises me how little information on necromancy is available outside of a few overpriced hard covers and the odd forum post here and there. Most have an edginess sharp enough to cut your eyeballs on, and no real substance either. The books which do contain useful ideas seem to be cursed with limited runs, putting the less experienced adepts off before they have even begun.

This seems to be something of a right of passage that forces each individual seeker to piece together their practice from whatever sources they found along the way. Perhaps that is how the Reaper prefers those who walk beside her to begin their studies, as scavengers and not scholars. Either way a little knowledge is a dangerous thing, so perhaps it is best to share as much as I can and hopefully mitigate some of that risk.

As once physical beings the wandering dead remember what they once where, and what was lost as their bodies returned to the soil. They are naturally attracted to certain physical and emotional residues, aspects of their being that now seem to be a distant and unobtainable dream. The exact form this craving takes will depend on what the spirit or ghostform clung to in life, though a few types of stimuli are universal.

The adept need only look to the mythology and folklore of the world to see the connection between the mechanics of physicality and the ever hungry dead. In *The Odyssey* animal blood is offered to the shade of Tiresias in exchange for prophecy, and the life force within it proved to be so attractive to those residing in the underworld that the swarm of starving souls could barely be held back by the hero's sword.

Further evidence of the power that such calidum sanguis holds over the dead can also be seen in the various vampire legends from across the globe. Regardless of the overt form that revenant takes or its temperament towards humankind, the majority of tales seem to agree that the living must be drained for these not quite dead to remain mobile within the material world. The blood is the life it seems, but as unholy as can be.

Of course, in matters of magick the necromancer should only use their own blood. Animal sacrifice has its place in some quasi-religious rites, but in general so little is needed to get the attention of the dead at certain locations that any more than a few drops is a waste. If focussed on the task the adept should have no trouble making contact with something eventually, though this is rarely the someone they were looking for.

Skeletal remains have a storied history as both tools by which the dead can be made to speak with the living and a home for visiting entities of various kinds. Human femurs are often depicted in woodcuts of older necromantic rites, likely because they were relatively straight and easy to carve for ritual. Skulls see use in witchcraft to this day, not only while speaking with ancestors but also as a general key to piercing the Veil.

And not forgetting finger bones, which were thrown to foretell the future or carved into talismans too. While purists may argue that human remains are the only viable type for this kind of once taboo conversation, in truth animal remains work just as well. The skull, as seat of both the personality and intelligence, is still the best choice for more mediumistic activities, true. But fox, wolf, cat or raven will do just fine.

For those who are dead set on acquiring human bones, the first consideration is one of local law. Some regions have strict guidelines on how these should be sourced, though in most cases both archaeological and ex-medical specimens are legal. Provenance is key though, as the decompositional processes and colour of the soil can stain a relatively recent, grave robbed skull, thereby making it look far older than it really is.

It goes without saying that any remains purchased under false pretences will cause problems in the adepts living space, be it by refusing to allow for targeted communication with the other side or general poltergeist like effects. Should these extend to the movement of lit candles or charcoal disks there is no telling how much damage could be done. As such animal bones, uncooked of course, are by far the safest option.

Of course other physical factors can attract the spirit world towards the still living too. Chronic pain, be it from damaged nerves or arthritic joints weakens the bioelectric field and pokes holes in the auric sheath that wail like alarm bells to anything that is drifting around looking for an easy meal. The adept can patch these by feeding on the energy of others, though the underlying issue must be dealt with for them to truly heal.

The lack of sleep caused by such constant, nagging pain can further weaken the target, not only making them more susceptible to psychic attack but the prolonged attention of astral parasites of various kinds as well. Advice on how to mitigate these sharp stabs of swirling fire is best left to trained medical professionals, though. Self medication can lead to addiction, and that has its own potential draw to certain ghostforms too.

It is rare to see a spirit return to comfort the sick or injured, though a few such stories of semitransparent nurses do exist within modern ghost lore. The reasoning for their presence tends towards the overly romantic, stating that they are staying around in penance for the patients they could not save while alive. A rare positive posthumous occupation to be sure, and hardly representative of their long dead ilk.

At opposite ends of the spectrum, both puberty and old age have their fair share of ghost stories. Children under six or so seem to attract the attentions of imaginary friends, usually docile but occasionally a divisive influence upon the wider family. The only way to shake these unwanted house guests free seems to be convincing the child to ignore them, and they eventually drift away to find attention elsewhere.

With teenagers it tends to be poltergeist type manifestations. While it would be convenient to chalk this one up to some form of manic ghostform or echo taking advantage of the biological changes and spiking bioelectric field, the argument that it is the emotionally overwrought mind of the adolescent themselves which causes the disturbances has been all but proven in the literature of psychical research.

The interaction between the old and the dead is a little more complicated, however, especially if they are on an extended stay in a hospice or nursing home. These are already thin places, seeing as they do the regular travel of residents across the Veil, and it can be safely assumed that not everyone who passes there will cross in full. Echoes and shards are rife in such environments, and the ghostforms tend to be especially well fed.

It is interesting to note that the wandering dead are also attracted to overly religious households, and it can be assumed that this is why so many Christian families claim a haunted status. Of course, by viewing this interaction through their prevailing paradigm, one which casts the entire supernatural realm as inhabited by fallen angels instead of ex-humans, they ruin any chance of being able to actually fight those spirits off.

Forum posts and social media tall tales all seem to tell the same story, highlighting how having a priest over to sprinkle some holy water and thump the Bible a few times in each room rarely has as much of an effect as when a local witch or medium comes over to drag the errant entity out of the basement by its ear. Polarity is key here, as what works on the infernal rarely effects the damned. The adept must know their enemy.

Of course not every fight is worth the effort. Considering just how attractive the magickal community are to astral entities of all kinds, and wandering ghostforms in particular, it may be best to politely decline an invitation to trip the darkness on their behalf in the first place. This is especially true where strangers and those outside of the esoteric or Neopagan spheres are involved.

Shards, which are just recurring psychic projections and place memories hanging in the air, will run down over time anyway. If the attentions of an echo, the malformed and animalistic imprint of a once living mind free floating in a perpetual state of hunger for negative or sorrowful energy of any type, is suspected to be involved then abstinence and cleaner living is the best advice that the adept can give the uninitiated anyway.

Necromancers in general have enough to be getting along with, and have no reason to go out looking for the kinds of trouble that might lead to criminal charges and loss of reputation. Being publicly outed as a priest or priestess of the Veil can and will change the adept's life in potentially damaging ways. When in doubt it is best to stay out of the line of fire and hope the balance will swing back in the victims favour on its own.

Current Ecology

As a calling that demands as much mental fortitude as it does physical prowess, walking along the cemetery path could be rightly considered an imaginative discipline. Each adept will naturally gravitate towards different aspects of the journey, and bring that unique worldview to colour the information that they pass along to the next generation before the anticipated return to Tiamat's womb.

My unique contribution to the death current is by giving form to function. The natural processes of decay are far easier to interface with on an esoteric level when they are seen as creatures in their own right. And weirdly enough, the pseudo-spirits that I have coalesced are now being seen by others in the wild, albeit under many different names. In fact, after reading this, they may well follow you through the graveyard too.

The accelerated necromancer lives in a world of spirits. As befits a path that calls upon shamanic Neopaganism as readily as the ritualistic diversity of chaos magick, theirs is the excesses of creation writ large on the local environment. But much of the ecology of the death current is open for interpretation, lending itself to personal cosmologies which help achieve the desired result with the minimum of fuss.

This selection is not arbitrary, however. All of the following pseudo-entities find their genesis within real world processes or otherworldly influences that the adept will need to navigate through regardless of how they choose to name and claim those forces. As such there is no need to draw a line between the classical view of the supernatural and this postmodern incarnation. Both can be of use, and at the same time too.

Ultimately the necromancer's success when dealing with these mostly adversarial presences will depend upon both their innate tenacity and hard won experience, nether of which grow in a vacuum. This haunted menagerie stands with the explorer by the graveside, their lilting siren song carried through the swirling mist from long dead lungs. It is best to be prepared before heeding that call, however.

Bone Eaters

An egregore of sorts cast from the various non-sentient processes that accompany bodily decomposition as well as the bacterial and insect level intelligences which profit from the corpse, bone eaters are hardly the cleverest pseudo-entities in the cemetery. That said the energy which flares up and then releases once the majority of the decay subsides is stable enough to hold a temporary spirit all its own for a short while.

This, then, is the essence that is encapsulated within the squirming and slimy landmine of decay just waiting to be siphoned off and put to work, perhaps through the charging of new iron nails driven into the site of the burial and left until the soil stops humming. Completely harmless and fleeting in nature, it is a perfect example of something that lacks classical sentience while still having slight agency in the material world.

Broken Dryads

Created from a malformed blending of both the nature and death currents within a single gnarled trunk, broken dryads are born when the elemental spirits usually tied to trees within leafy forest glades are recast through a much colder, graveyard lens. With a sickly yet persistent essence that is amply reflected in their name, and branches that whisper horsely on even the stillest summer day, they are easy enough to spot.

Having roots set down in any number of surrounding burials, leeching the remaining nutrients from within those now forgotten caskets, also leads to an intriguing side effect where the tree drinks up some of the shards remaining within the soil as well. Rarely hostile despite this fragmented personality, these lanterns of living decay can provide the adept with a safe place to sit and rest between other, more dangerous tasks.

Echoes

An astral nuisance usually found in cemeteries, echoes linger to siphon off the emotions of those paying their respects to deceased loved ones. Sorrow and loss are the drip feed that keeps these extremely limited pseudo-entities from dissipating completely, though some will choose to range farther afield and become what the public know as poltergeists, switching their diet to adolescent angst and family fears instead.

Interestingly even just the pretence of a personality is missing here. All that remains is animalistic hunger and the numbing lethargy which comes from essentially being lobotomised during the mental projection process, one which spawned them instead of a fully functional ghostform. While they can be spoken to by the adept, and may well answer, there is unlikely to be much truth within those incoherent words.

Graveyard Guardians

By far the most intriguing pseudo-entities within the ecology of the graveyard, these protective forces work something like unreal antibodies, keeping those who would pollute the gardens of the dead at bay. While rarely seen visually they may be responsible for the persistent association between burial plots and ghostly monks. They do indeed appear this way, though others look more like a large shuck than a cowled friar.

Folklore ties them to the first burial within the grounds, cursed to protect the remains of those who came after until not even dust remains. This is incorrect, as they are actually an expression of the oversoul of the collective inhabitants of the location instead, jealously draining the bioelectric field of interlopers should they try to disrupt its harmony. They can be appeased with ritual, or when the adept claims the cemetery.

Shards

Responsible for many of the static apparitions which are regularly seen within wood panelled great halls or medieval churches, shards are little more than fragments of memory that are accidentally played back by naturally skilled, though usually unaware, members of the public. Of such things, ghost stories are made, though few would want to admit that their own tall tale was really down to a non-sentient recording.

As to how such images are formed, they rarely seem to stem from the usual violent or unexpected passing which would release a ghostform or echo into the world. No, these are usually far more banal in nature, describing times of longing and stress instead. Likely just psychic leakage during life their existence has little bearing on the necromancer's attempt to keep the balance, or the wider death current in general.

Shucks

Named after the massive crossroad psychopomps that dominate old English folklore, in the narrower context of accelerated necromancy other fleeting and secretive entities share the title alongside the usual saucer eyed, midnight black canines. Indeed any of the various incorporeal but roughly mammalian shapes who dart between the bushes also count as a part of that grouping, albeit out of expediency if nothing else.

Far from unintelligent, the adept will likely find themselves being tracked or at least travelling alongside these furtive watchers when harvesting ingredients, especially during twilight when the natural shadows are missing. Be they the left over ghostforms of once living animals or the sorrow of pet owners projected forwards after their furry companion's death, there is little to fear from their admittedly unnerving dance.

A Quick And Dirty Banishing

Often when visiting historical locations outside of a formalised ghost hunting session I will run into something that was just as surprised to see me there as I was to feel their presence. And the reaction from their side is usually pretty toxic. Tides of hate and fear roll off such resident ghostforms in undulating waves, and can easily overwhelm the tired adept.

Only once have I let such things cause me to stumble in my step, and it was soon rebuffed in kind. For those fleeting few moments though, where I was forced to return to the corridor to catch a breath before re-entering the room all guns blazing, I felt what the average person does when faced with haunted homes. To be fair I had been awake for almost three days at that point, though it is no excuse for such weakness.

Not all ghosts are encountered during overnight vigils. Hotel rooms, restaurants, even rented chalets are all just as likely to harbour a resident haunt. And considering that the necromancer may not always keep a fully stocked knapsack with them during their downtime, or have the opportunity to pull out foxfire and incense while travelling with the general public, an open handed ritual is instead required.

As such, this deceptively simple visualisation exercise allows the accelerated adept to clear their immediate space without falling back on more intensive auric defence techniques, while also setting up a barrier that prevents anything else from moving back into the vacuum which is created after the quick and dirty banishing is performed in a given location as well.

The core idea revolves around filling instead of emptying the room, and pushing whatever was once in there back through the walls to bother someone else. This is far easier than direct conflict with pseudo-entities that will likely have the home turf advantage in those situations, while also being simple enough to be performed in even the most tired or stressed of mental states as well.

No preparation is needed, though the effectiveness of a quick and dirty banishing is limited by the space that will need to be covered to fully clear a room. Especially large or vaulted locations such as churches or Tube tunnels are a difficult shape to fully expand into, and the presence of a large group of agitated people will also cause problems too. That said it is always worth a try, as no harm will come to anyone should it fail.

The adept starts by using their minds eye to draw the image of a pentagram in front of them, about six inches from their skin, beginning and ending in the bottom left corner. The colour is not important, only that it seems to burn with some form of white hot essence, smouldering brands of the necromancer's indomitable will searing into the flesh of the astral and allowing no reprisal from that direction.

A second is imagined behind. Then a third to the left and forth to the right before one is visualised in contact with the feet and another above the head. Once held in the psychic space around the adept for a few seconds, all are set to spin, slow at first but gathering pace until they are little better than quickly shifting circles which seem to have lost their original pointed form.

The necromancer then tenses up for a moment, before relaxing and in doing so sends those disks of pure imaginative essence in all previously mentioned directions, effectively creating a fast moving invisible box with them at its core, one that will mould itself to the contours of the room and blend with the physical boundaries of the space. And of course, it applies the searing, ever spinning pentagrams as it does so.

While not a permanent solution the fire and forget nature of the quick and dirty banishing will allow for a quiet nights sleep or uneventful visit to an unexpectedly haunted place, though should more than one application be required during a longer stay then other methods are probably more energy efficient over a protracted period of time.

When The Fun Stops

It goes without saying that not everything encountered outside of the ritual chamber will be friendly. I have come up against immaterial resistance to my presence more than once over the years, usually in untended graveyards or storied stately homes, and been forced to fall back on less than poetic methods to keep myself and those around me safe.

More so than a religious choice, Accelerated Necromancy is really just a skill set. And as with any truly rounded discipline there are failsafes in place should the worst happen and a good time go bad. Bloodymindedness and a strong will can only get you so far, after all. Sometimes it is better to quite visibly carry the big stick rather than bother with the pretence of walking softly anyway.

Back when I was an amateur ghost hunter, and likely the only Neopagan in the room, I often took a knapsack full of very specific tricks with me just in case the shadows decided to bite back. And now, by following the examples listed below, you can be just as prepared for when the lights fade out too.

The Panic Room

While useful to the more experienced adept, the following technique is also deliberately geared towards newer practitioners who might have genuine problems dealing with the sometimes far from subtle energies which can be released when exploring the unseen world. It is also aimed more at those who spend their free time inside abandoned locations rather than supposedly haunted historical buildings.

The more social necromancer may well end up carrying others through situations which could be considered to be negative alarmingly often, especially in the age of internet influencers and amateur ghost hunting groups.

Few seasoned paranormal investigators would willingly work with those who profess to seek the Veil of course, though are also unlikely to refuse the help when the night bumps back.

This is not a blanket judgement of those who would knowingly put themselves in harm's way to experience the weird, however. There is much to gain from resurrecting old urban legends or summoning the dead for kicks either alone or with friends, especially outside of organised or paid groups.

In some small towns, and the run down rookeries that pad out the poorer parts of otherwise opulent cities, hanging around in dark and desolate ruins from sunset to dawn could even be seen as a rite of passage. But accidents happen, and they are far more likely when those present are spiralling into paranoid chaos without a safety valve to relieve the pressure.

Violent confrontations with the actual dead or occasionally demonic are extremely uncommon, and it is more likely the group itself that will cause the issue unless given a suitably designated place to catch a breath. Much of the pomp and ceremony involved in the panic room is designed to soothe that human element, while still keeping any external forces at bay as well.

Relying on the inherent power within self defined sacred spaces and a handful of items from the necromancer's knapsack, the panic room as a physical construct is designed to remain both quick to set up and easy to tear down after use. It also shades into classical occult ideas such as ritual circles and area wards while leaving little trace after removal. Plus it looks quite impressive to the uninitiated too.

The first thing to consider is the choice of room. Ideally it should be of small to medium size, comfortably furnished and able to accommodate the entire group with easy, obstacle free access from the place of investigation. That means no stairs, no locked doors and very little intervening furniture either.

This initial decision is much easier should the adept have a chance to scout out the building ahead of time in line with the P7 protocol, though the actual creation of the panic room can still be undertaken after the ectoplasm has firmly hit the fan due to how little effort it actually requires to get up and running.

The ability to receive a strong mobile phone signal once inside with all the access doors closed is important, as is the precaution of letting at least one other person who will not be in attendance know where the adept is intending to be that evening. This remains true even if the actual reasons are kept ambiguous due to conflicting spiritual beliefs.

Such a lifeline becomes mandatory when the necromancer decides to conduct a solo investigation in unfamiliar or derelict surroundings, including remote woodland and abandoned commercial properties too. These are the kind of places where bodies tend to go undiscovered for months at a time if a dedicated search and rescue presence is not pointed directly at the area of interest from the outset, after all.

All windows and curtains should be closed prior to the setting up of the panic room. Any mirrors should be covered or removed to another part of the building so that they will not act as potential access points for undesirable entities into the otherwise sealed chamber. This also prevents hysterical members of the group causing further stress when they claim to see something reflected in the glass.

The entire inside edge of the room should be drawn out with foxfire salts, if the adept is carrying enough in their knapsack to do so, to form a thin unbroken line running along the floor as close to the walls as possible. Stick chalk can also be used to scribe this barrier, though does not always cover all surfaces and will be far less effective on dirt or damp trash.

This boundary line is then extended across the opening between the door frame and the door, leaving a small gap to allow people to enter the sacred space without disrupting its outer edge or metaphysical integrity. A crown of thorns can be looped over the top of the frame if one has been prepared ahead of time, and allowed to dangle down between the uprights too.

Incense should then be lit on a sturdy table in the centre of the room, away from the door, and small tealights placed in stable holders around them. Neither of these need be consecrated, unless the adept wishes to make the extra effort, and on the rare occasions that the building restricts the use of open flames a bowl of pungent dried herbs can be poured next to a couple of battery powered candles instead.

Frankincense smoke is especially good for banishing unwanted energies, and myrrh has a long history of use alongside this for a similar result. Garlic salt is great as a base of a dry blend, along with sage and iron filings if the latter are available. And of course any left over foxfire works wonders as well.

Both the atmosphere they create and the effect that has to bolster the spirits of the group are the main considerations here. It is always worth remembering that at its most basic level the point of the panic room is simply to calm and reassure those present. Only when working solo in a potentially active place do those added aesthetic qualities loose their value, as the adept has little to gain from tricking themselves.

Necromancers in general are at least indifferent to the same fear which plagues the uninitiated during explorations into supposedly haunted locations, and some even seem to thrive upon it. With that in mind they are more likely to have a few handy banishing tools in their knapsack for mobile use as opposed to a specially constructed bolt hole to retreat inside.

Plus their ongoing relationship with their own Jungian shadow, the internalised ghostform that is given room to grow and develop within their waking world, also makes it less likely that anything nasty from the unseen realm will be able to latch on to them anyway. The general public, however, are not similarly shielded against the astral parasites in their midst.

After the initial set up panic room scenario is open for personal interpretation depending upon the spiritual beliefs of those inside. Small statues of patron deities, crosses, rosaries, holy books, grimoires, runic symbols, chalices. Anything which holds a positive association for those assembled can be added to the table, and no items of significance should be refused a place as long as they will safely fit.

While some may be enamoured with the idea of scribing pentagrams or other protective symbols on the walls or windows with either spray paint or just the chalk itself, to do so breaks the golden rule of urban exploration. Take only pictures, leave only footprints. So no, even the threat of facing down the dead is no excuse for petty vandalism.

Once the room is needed the gap in the chalk or foxfire line running across the entrance is closed and the door shut over it. This seals the sacred space from outside energies, though anyone stepping over the threshold the accelerated necromancer has created, in either direction, will render it useless.

Again, any prayers or banishing rituals that the group wishes to take part in at this point may prove useful, though far from essential. It is unlikely that the adept will get much sleep after such an emotionally turbulent evening, but it should be safe enough to do so as long as someone is always keeping at least half an eye on the candles to make sure they do not catch any of the other items in the room on fire.

Home at sunrise then, once the location is better lit and safer to traverse. Hopefully those assembled will be calmer by that point too, and this will reduce the risk of tripping or falling into the more derelict spaces within the building while leaving. The dead rarely attack the living, of course, but that does not stop the idea of them doing so causing very physical harm among panicked people.

Indeed it is almost unheard of for a small group of teens taking part in a rite of passage at an abandoned warehouse to actually run into anything truly dangerous. There may be ghostforms, echoes or shards there, true, but aside from the odd fleeting shadow or strange noise in the far distance it is fear itself that can cause the most harm to those who have no experience seeking out the weird.

This is less of a consideration for commercial ghost hunts, usually due to the lack of any real activity in the massively overhyped and annoyingly pristine historical locations. So unless made aware otherwise ahead of time there is no need for the necromancer to bring much with them aside from the usual contents of their knapsack, as keeping others safe by spell and showmanship in those situations is not really a concern.

Auric Armour

No necromancer is an island, nor adept a small principality. As such there will be occasions when they come up against something or someone who needs to be reminded about personal autonomy in a far from subtle, but still ostensibly legal, way.

And while it is seen as little better than a background hum in some traditions, I have found the aura to be a hugely versatile tool that can rebuff most minor threats with little effort. Yes, balance is a key drive for those who seek to approach the Veil. But no one ever said that a proportional response was against the rules.

As a path that recognises the life force inherent in all things, accelerated necromancy is uniquely suited to manipulating those tiny bursts of bioelectricity into something truly magickal. And as with most techniques the first step towards encoding this internal reservoir of psychic force into something useful is the ability to feel its presence.

While the bone glow ritual is a viable method to explore the internal scaffolding within the mortal shell, by far the best way to interface with the energetic sheath that sits a millimetre or so around it is during a warm bath. This is because the added sensation of water surrounding the entire body helps to focus the attention onto both the top layer of skin and through to the lower dermal strata via the radiated heat.

Once this dull tingle is recognised the adept can then begin drawing lines and swirls through it with their mind, pinching and pulling their focus in places until enough control is gained to attempt the next stage of the work. This is similar, but conducted nude and dry, and concludes once the same level of surface level manipulation is achieved.

After repeated reinforcement the necromancer will become familiar enough with the workings of their own bioelectric field for it to then become possible to not only begin encoding it with purpose through focussed visualisation but also access those abilities when both clothed and in motion too.

This may sound far-fetched, but it is an undeniably real skill that can be learned through both practice and a suspension of disbelief. Because if the spark of life coursing through the aura is used to power servitors and birth tulpas, pseudo-entities created from sculpted mind stuff and loosed into the world, then infusing that astral sheath with a similar informational bundle suddenly becomes a very intriguing idea.

The most talked about passive psychic defence is the mirror shield. This is simple to create, and only requires the adept to imagine the bioelectric field resembling a glassy surface, something akin to a second skin of liquid metal that reflects the negativity back at those dishing it out.

While widely used, this technique is in truth massively flawed. Pushing back against an attacker with their own aggression can cause the situation to escalate exponentially where it would otherwise die down. It is unlikely that the uninitiated would be able to taste their own emotions being returned to them, after all, instead seeing the reflected malice as originating with their suddenly defiant victim instead.

The naturally empathic who fall back on mirror shielding out of necessity have likely witnessed such an emotional death spiral first hand, and the only way to de-escalate the quickly brewing conflict is to retreat. That is not to say the idea is without any merit, however, as it works extremely well as a glamour spell of sorts instead.

While not specifically defensive, the ability to replicate the underlying characteristics of a given group may well be one of the main reasons why many more experienced adepts still bother to use the technique. Be it an important interview or a quickly brewing riot, anything which tips the events towards a positive outcome should not be ignored no matter how rudimentary it at first appears.

Instead of a mirror, embracing the shadows that naturally gather as the sun or moon illuminate the landscape is far more useful. The best armour is avoidance, and blending into the background makes the adept a far less obvious target for both the living and the dead alike.

This is literally as easy as standing in a shadow and pulling the absence of light up into the aura through focussed will, until the adept visualises themselves as fully obscured, a cold shiver signalling the successful completion of the operation. Imagining a large cog or fan blade spinning over the heart but beneath their ribs as it draws the swirling darkness in through the hands and feet can also help focus at this stage.

As for results, this does not grant invisibility, of course, more a hazy mental cloud that causes observers to just lose interest. So coupled with bland clothes and a small crowd milling around the skilled adept can move safely through most urban environments, drawing little attention from the average inhabitants as they go about their magickal business.

It also works quite well when walking around an adopted graveyard looking for supplies in secret, though does not stop any guardian spirits who might be looking for trespassers. The elemental entities and hungry ghost-forms which populate such locations cannot be so easily fooled.

Once the necromancer becomes confident in pulling the darkness into their bioelectric field they then gain access to an energetic shout of sorts, a silent scream of rage and pain which also works as well against the living as the dead. Using this methodology a target can easily be rebuffed by a quick burst of negative emotion channelled first into the aura and then out towards them through the intervening space.

Touch may seem to be the best vector here, but is not recommended due to the potential legal ramifications stemming from such physical contact. Plus if striking the aggressor anyway then there is no point in trying to add magick into the mix. Hit hard, hit fast, and move on.

Due to the potential ferocity of this technique it is a very bad idea to argue with a necromancer while they are standing in a graveyard. It would be all too easy for the sorcerer to shunt the energies of death and decomposition into their aura instead of the shadows and pulse it towards their enemies when surrounded by human remains in such abundance.

Such focussed death rattle never proves deadly, true, but all does add nicely to the adept's assumed air of miasmic horror. This can be further built upon to create something of a necrotic glamour when the priest or priestess of the Veil would prefer to be left alone to conduct their usually solemn business in peace. Hardly charming, but undeniably effective regardless.

That said, if remaining inconspicuous is of less concern to the adept than immediate defensive considerations then a purely mechanical methodology presents itself. And of all the techniques designed to raise their shields against incoming spiritual or emotional assault mentioned so far, this is the only one that will work for those who have no background in magick as well.

Exercise is the key here. A quick burst of mildly strenuous activity is enough to increase blood flow, and release copious amounts of testosterone. Both of these, coupled with the rise in body temperature, will help to energise the veins and tissues which support the bioelectric field and aid it in becoming impenetrable to weaker outside stimuli.

Be aware, however, that if the necromancer chooses to step themselves up a gear or two in this way it comes with the caveat that they will also begin to shine like a lantern in the moonlight. For that reason such showboating should be avoided if the perceived threat is a particularly negative ghost-form or similar pseudo-entity who might want to chase down the free meal in their midst.

In general the adept should only travel to the places of the dead once they are confident in the metaphysical armour that they move within. And far from being heavy salted steel or nimble blessed leather, it is instead the very energy which flows within their mortal frame that remains the best defence against those seeking to do them harm.

Ghoulish Hunger

I am very aware of my place in the world. I accept that my physical shell is only maintained through the sacrifice of others and as a result it is not uncommon to hear me thank the spirit of the animal whose meat I am about to consume for their sacrifice, or the trees for their fruit.

Cherishing my current material existence I am willing to fall back on any and all survival methods should the situation call for drastic action. Even those considered taboo. And when the need arises to recharge my bioelectric batteries after a particularly chaotic week I feed in decidedly ghoulish ways.

Like all living things, the necromancer is dependent on consuming others to survive. Animals mostly, and plants too, though should a particularly desperate adept seek instead to feast on human prey there are methods which allow them to do so without causing permanent harm. And no, it does not involve disinterring or otherwise interfering with the remains of the dead.

For while outsiders may draw obvious parallels with the taboo discipline of vampirism the adept need not fall back on fangs to seek sustenance in this way. No blood, no pain for themselves or others. The true power lies in encoding the aura with weaponised shadows, a natural next step for those who have mastered their bioelectric field.

Of course, before moving on to the living, those wishing to learn the intricacies of this ghoulish feeding should instead start with the shards available in their local cemetery. Fragments of energy left over from the corpses interred below, and externally projected slices of memory from those visiting them above, these necromantic pseudo-spirits are really just a free meal for the suitably skilled.

The non-sentient nature of those lesser bundles of incoherent but perhaps visually intriguing information renders them fair game for the budding adept when they seek to step off of the cemetery path for a while to grab some lunch. And those endlessly repeating apparitions are a heady, if uniquely chilled, stew of astral debris with a taste like no other.

Such absorption is the simplest form of ghoulish feeding, and the one best suited to situations where the necromancer needs to self medicate with the minimum of fuss. The methodology is reassuringly simple, as once the adept is comfortable in altering the informational makeup of their bioelectric field the aura becomes a powerful tool for open handed magick of all kinds.

While resting on a shady bench in an older part of the cemetery the necromancer closes their eyes and performs a quick bone glow ritual to help ground them in the current moment. Once this is over, the shadows under the seat are visualised as being pulled into the aura through focussed imagination, and a cool shiver running down their spine will show that this has been completed correctly.

As with the more defensive shadow aura technique, a quickly spinning whirlpool can be imagined beneath the ribs and over their heart while the chosen energetic signature is drawn up through the hands and feet. A yammering mouth full of jagged teeth is then visualised over and around their abdomen, though this will not be used just yet.

Once enough darkness is circulating within the bioelectric field the absence of light is imagined as changing into a spongy mass similar to low quality sack cloth, open weave and loose fitting over the necromancer's auric sheath. This is then willed to absorb the loose energy and memories floating by like a sponge in blood.

The essence that is drawn in will have a chill to it, of course, and regardless of time of year or layers of clothing that uncomfortable feeling will build as the spaces between the randomly woven strands of shadow just millimetres above the skin begin to soak up the collected debris that make up the atmosphere of the graveyard.

This passive absorption is designed to mirror the method by which the loosely associated informational mass that makes up the not quite body of a wandering echo feeds upon the energy in a given area, turning heat to cold as it does so. But the necromancer is willingly reversing that process, taking that deathly chill and eventually returning it to healing warmth through cellular activity.

Particularly mediumistic adepts will pick up images or hear voices, fragments of the lives that have been interred beneath the soil around them and the sorrow of those who visit the graves of loved ones now lost to the Veil.

This can be interesting, true, but is merely a side effect of the digestion of the stray essence as it trickles into the ever hungry abdominal maw. Those insights are of no real consequence.

Taken to its extreme a close quarters version of this technique can be used as a form of folk exorcism, though it is not easy to keep the restless dead in place long enough to take anything more than a small snippet of energy at a time. Thought forms can also be dissolved in this way if desired, and room clearings completed if the adept is hungry enough to empty the astral fridge all in one go.

Echoes which have become merged with the auric field of a still living victim are far easier to force into a corner, however. Historically considered to have been reduced in death to animalistic expressions of whatever concept most occupied them in life they seek out still living souls who share that obsession, becoming spectral parasites existing vicariously through the experiences of their hosts.

While abstinence might be the best method for removing these pseudo-spirits in the long term, a skilled necromancer can also try to dislodge them with a swift auric kick. Consuming the essence of such a negative astral leech is not generally considered to be disrespectful towards the dead. Through their actions it is safe to assume that they had it coming.

Most followers of the necromantic path would never seek to deliberately harm spirits of any kind without direct provocation and as such prefer passive feeding over such combative techniques. The energetic signature which holds those wandering entities together is just too fragile, and the disruption caused by a particularly voracious adept would risk unravelling them wholesale.

The living, however, can always stand to lose a few bites worth of bioelectricity without being put in any true danger. All that is needed is a little visualisation and a lot of potential targets, though an ability to maintain fully animated auric programming while moving is also a plus.

And yes, this is a more militant version of the same thing that magickians and witches from a number of unrelated disciplines have sought to do when skimming off some of the stray energy at rock concerts or dance clubs to keep on their feet until dawn. The only difference is one of degree, as it does not require those victims to be in a heightened state at all.

Once the necromancer is in a suitable location, such as a rush hour train station or busy weekend high street, they pull the shadows into themselves through the hands and feet as before. Minds eye images of both the spinning heart whirlpool and toothy abdominal maw perfected earlier will also be required for success.

Turning the aura to absorbent sack cloth is not enough here. The living are too well defended to release enough energy into the atmosphere around them for that methodology to be of use while going about their every day lives. No, like the voracious wolf spider that they are the adept will need to unfurl great arachnid limbs cast from the absence of light and poke a hole or two of their own.

No one will ever see them of course. The necromancer only perceives those ever striking appendages with their psychic senses and as part of the visualisation portion of the ghoulish feeding ritual, half watching them as they return with their bioelectric spoils to be deposited in the chattering mental maw which drips shadowy ichor from over their abdomen.

As a sovereign being with hard won control over the energetic information which makes up their auric shields the adept is free to sculpt those bladed feeding tools in any way they wish. Tentacles, extra arms, swirling intestines or creaking bone. As long as they stay attached to the body at the root any and all of these should be viable.

That is an important consideration, however. Any attempts to create autonomous feeding implements, such as swarms of black butterflies or toothy balls of ulcerated shadow flesh will likely fail due to being separated from the auric sheath which powers them. Servitors and tulpas would work better for that kind of long range work, though are far more costly from an energetic standpoint than the food they would carry back.

For the more sceptical among the necromantic community these flashier aspects of the feeding process can be treated as little more than a mental scaffold created to bolster the adept's attempts to steal the energy of those around them through otherwise undefined means. Internalised ritual, perhaps. A morality play with fangs and ever present hunger. Weaponised delusion. Fantasy as fact, yet the results speak for themselves.

This does not matter either way, because as long as they get the pick me up they need to carry on along their cemetery path then the how is far less important than the outcome. The aura repaired, hunger satiated, one foot in front of the other as the shadows close in. And the Reaper smiling from her seat upon the nearest tombstone, happy to be denied her prize for yet another day.

Sharing The Meal

Not all of the knowledge that I have gained while walking along this cemetery path was painless in its acquisition. No one who seeks the Veil will be doing so out of pure curiosity, as the price of carrying those mental and physical energies is just too high for the legend tripper or plastic adept to handle. Death is an ever present companion on this journey, and demands that we face it down, sorrow and all.

As with many who explore the fringes of the esoteric sphere for decade after decade there is an ever growing list of those who I was ultimately unable to save, no matter how much they mattered to me. I did not always try of course, but when the motivation to act was strong enough the very gods themselves looked on in wonder at my will. A bold statement, though such forthright action made little difference in the end.

Projection, the art of healing others, remains a mostly overlooked aspect within the wider necromantic paradigm. An inversion of the auric feeding techniques which the adept can use to keep themselves pushing forward during physically difficult times, these far less invasive visualisations utilise the same underlying ritual structure but blunt all those teeth and tentacles towards more altruistic ends instead.

Especially useful when curled up close to a loved one, if correctly applied this ghoulish healing allows the necromancer's own bioelectric field to overlap and envelop that of the target, instinctively identifying and reinforcing the areas damaged by injury or disease. Visualising the auric sheath as a shifting skin of loose threads akin to sack cloth can help to do this, though any spongy and porous imagery works just as well.

Success will rely upon the adept's ability to read the energy levels of those close to them, and feel the difference in resistance that healthy and wounded bioelectric fields will create. Once identified the necromancer begins to will their own aura to envelop that of their target, small needle-like stitches or sutures knitting together the rips and tears that are causing the recipient fatigue or pain.

This is not a cure however, and will not remove the underlying medical condition no matter how skilled an auric surgeon the priest or priestess of the Veil becomes. These visualised stitches are best viewed as a tailor made unreal bandages, a transference of healthy energy to fill the void caused by more pressing health problems while waiting for actual professional advice. It works especially well on toothache too.

Unfortunately it can only ever provide short term relief for longer term issues, as the aura will soon begin to fall into a state of decay again unless that proper flesh and blood repair is undertaken. Also, while the energy of others will dull the pain of the sufferer this all too brief respite will only prolong their overall agony should the condition be untreatable. Sadly, sometimes dead is indeed better after all.

Be under no illusions, chronic or terminal conditions will require regular applications to keep the recipient ticking away, though it is desirable that the necromancer either rest between rituals to regain their own strength or take time to siphon off the energy of others through ghoulish feeding instead. Regardless this entire area of the art is dangerously close to upsetting the balance, and moderation is key.

If death is on the horizon then the priest or priestess of the Veil should leave the Reaper to her work, steadfastly refusing to interfere unless personal connections force them to do so. When this is the case a much more desperate and hazardous version of the previous technique can be utilised. This is ghoulish straddling, and it tends to have serious consequences for all involved,

Designed to help mitigate dire conditions for a short time, long enough perhaps to give their final goodbyes to family who are travelling from elsewhere to get to the bedside of the terminal person and may be a while, it is not recommend unless all other options have already been exhausted. It does indeed work, and well enough to carry the load for a day or two, perhaps a week at most.

The adept seeks to bond their physical shell with that of their target, becoming a bio-electric battery attuned to those energetic needs at all times, even when many miles away. Part auric overlap, part astral tethering, the results can be surprisingly miraculous. There is a heavy price to pay, however, as the healer begins to sicken in sympathy and must constantly fight their own survival instincts to maintain the link.

The auric aspects of the operation are largely the same as with any other attempt at necromantic healing, though will require the person who is offering up their energy to allow some of the recipient's bioelectric field to intermingle and merge with their own beforehand. This is necessary so that neither side of the Faustian deal will experience rejection.

Once this is done the adept extends a long, writhing cable of focussed light forward from their belly button directly into the base of the spine of their loved one, giving them a direct connection to the necromancer's own reserves. Alternatively the connection can be created back to back and works the same, though both are extremely difficult unless there is some form of familial or otherwise personal connection between the two.

Constantly feeding the sick person life force in this way they will allow them to regain some of their original vitality, though never enough to effect a cure. Extremely draining and dangerous, the adept must accept that they may never recover fully from the strain that this puts upon their physical and spiritual reserves, especially if they also have a demanding day job or family life to deal with as well.

Either way any connections, ritualistic or otherwise, must be severed before the patient crosses the Veil. If this is not done successfully they may remain open indefinitely and irreversibly scar the bio-electric field of the adept as the death current itself finds a conduit into their physical shell. And no, as attractive as this may sound to some, it is a very bad idea to try and fail that last step on purpose.

A final note on outsourcing this sort of energetic scaffolding to the already dead. While such a stopgap measure may seem like a way around the strain of maintaining these energetic links long term, it is actually an extremely bad idea to point such astral parasites towards an already damaged aura under the pretence of offering healing in exchange for some form of pact or future favour.

The chthonic gods are equally unlikely to offer direct aid. There is always the danger of the necromancer leading astral leeches or vast and immutable psychopomps directly to someone already flying dangerously close to the Veil, and while this is a viable form of magickal assault it is obviously not a balanced action to instigate against someone the adept is supposed to care about.

BOOK THREE

The Dead Walk

As a necromancer I do not focus my withering gaze solely into the realms of the dead. More akin perhaps to the Earthen traditions of my neopagan past, the accelerated form of the art is intimately tied to the spirit of place. Because without that all important connection to the land which past generations lived and eventually died within, there is no hope of understanding their continued existence beyond the grave.

Realising this early on in my own journey along the cemetery path, likely because of my interest in urban exploring and long, rambling walks through rain slick streets, I decided to formalise those excursions. And with a little research I stumbled upon psychogeography, twisting that thoughtful interplay between city and population towards a new kind of necromantic ritual.

Above all else I sought to find a way to formalise that innate respect for the history of the urban sprawl, to seek bloodstains long painted over and pay my respects to the shades who may have known a very different city to the one that I currently inhabit. Because ultimately all towns are ghost towns, it is just that some are full of the living as well.

Necrogeography

By far the best method for understanding the haunted city is to walk freely and attentively within its storied boundaries. Origin and destination are largely unimportant, only the journey matters. While the Situationists and Letterists of the 20th Century saw such excursions as a form of resistance against what they considered to be a toxic environment, the necromancer instead seeks to embrace what has been built around them.

Layers, strata, accretions of time represented in the mundane materials of car park and alleyway. Living veins of architectural information bleeding history into the street as fibre optic cables pulse like a rolling seizures within the nervous system of the urban sprawl. Payphones and benches. A tiny window box worth of green. And all the while the dead reach up quizzically with gnarled fingers from beneath concrete slabs.

Necrogeography, related as it is to the concept of the dérive, or drift through the urban landscape, may have more of a focussed purpose than the dreamy and deliberately ungoverned walks of those earlier groups. But it definitely owes a debt to their pioneering work decontextualising and then recontextualising the austere landscape of postwar Europe through an intensely personal lens.

While it does exhibit a similar methodology to the wider discipline of psychogeography. this necromancer specific variation differs on one major point. It is not enough to vaguely interact with the landscape, to dwell within the feelings and emotions which those concrete and tarmac roads bring to the surface. It should never be a completely unexpected journey, nor should the desire to find the dead places within the city be denied.

Though intriguing insights can be drawn from the urban sprawl by simply allowing the flow of the streets to carry the adept like driftwood downstream towards uncertain shores, they also have to keep an eye on the signs left by the many thousands of lives that once occupied the route as well. Thus the big difference between those who walk the cemetery path and the Situationists of yesteryear becomes one of focal lens.

Taking those first steps on the necrogeographic journey may seem daunting at first. A major capitol such as London or New York is far too large to drink in all the immanent history in one go, while even the smallest cities can be densely packed around a swirl of commerce and administrative buildings many miles deep. As such, a method of carving up the built landscape is needed. A waypoint system of sorts.

The first stop for setting up such arbitrary markers will always involve looking into the nature of the city. Amateur historians, unrecognised antiquarians, or even occult authors with an interest in the many layers of life and death which have occurred where they live. The conceit of such titles is mostly irrelevant as yet another microfiche is loaded into the tray to display the newspapers and journals of a world that once was.

Local history, while occasionally sordid and almost uniformly violent, may not offer the necromancer any real points of interest. In these cases it is better to read of the ghostly tales and strange folklore said to be situated within the area instead. The truth of those narratives is not what is initially important. All that matters is that an anchor point in the built landscape is earmarked for future exploration.

Maps are useful here, as is an understanding of thin places and corpse ways too. Of course that latter designations will usually develop once streets with a particularly vibrant wellspring of the death current flowing through them have been traversed a few times, and a feel for the way the essence itself trickles like a sluggish and bracken choked river through the modernity that has grown up organically around it is gained.

In the interim before such experiential or even library learned knowledge has been assimilated into the wider historical worldview that the necromancer is starting to develop there are alternatives which are much easier to find. The whereabouts of graveyards and cemeteries are likely to already be well known to the adept, for example, and failing that county morgues or funeral homes can also work in a pinch.

The idea is not to find the perfect destination, but just to have a waypoint in mind during the ever drifting journey. A city is to be traversed, not idolised. Virtual representations are not good enough, and no matter how much is read about the murders, crime and perhaps even ghosts that are said to inhabit it after dark the truth must be felt brushing against the skin, tasted in the air. Experience is everything.

To begin the practical part of their necrogeographic ritual the adept sets out with a certain landmark in mind. This is not to be thought of as a definite destination, because doing so may limit the overall scope of the drift. It is instead seen for what it truly is, just an unremarkable space among so many others that will be encountered as the adept travels through the city while in a reverent and observant frame of mind.

And the urban sprawl will talk back, if the necromancer has the ears to listen. Stickers on lamp posts offer instruction on which street to take next. Signs in windows point to local landmarks and even the smell of fast food can draw the seeker ever further towards the insights which await them. Cracks in the pavement work as roughly etched runes, spelling out a vital message only a practitioner of the dérive can decipher.

Rubbish choked alleys and icy canal paths may be encountered, calling to all who are interested and telling tales of a bloody past. Places of murder and intrigue, ghost cars and phantom coaches. The numbing banality of prefabricated local government offices and excitement of stumbling upon a new monument or green space just waiting to be catalogued. If an effort is made to seek such locations then the city will provide.

Notepad, voice recorder. Regardless of the method chosen, when the adept feels the death current welling up in a certain location they should stop and make a note of where they are. This information can then be cross-referenced after the walk has concluded, to see if there was any known reason for such a strong pull. If not then a record should still be kept, just in case that particular spot comes up again in future walks.

This darkly liminal area is usually a graveyard, long forgotten plague pit or site of mass slaughter. Such open wounds in the fabric of the living world spill their necromantic essence into the streets all around. As these and similar locations pull the priest or priestess of the Veil onwards they may eventually make it to their original waypoint. A rest can be taken there, perhaps a bite of lunch and seat beneath leafy trees.

Yet not every drift will take the traveller anywhere near the location that had originally chosen, and there is nothing wrong with that. Multiple attempts may be required for the city to draw them to the place they seek. Yet each walk, if done in the correct spirit of open exploration, will still hold value. It is not a race to success, but an intimate relationship with the very flesh of the city itself that the necromancer seeks.

The waypoint is ultimately unimportant. Nothing but an arbitrary marker to give the illusion of progress and perhaps even success to an endeavour that in truth requires neither to be completed correctly. That said, once a long enough break has been taken there the dérive resumes in a random direction, until the drifting, ultra observant state of mind fades and it is realised that nothing new can be gained on this particular journey.

Home then, to hit the books and collate the results. Maps are updated with newly won knowledge. Journals copied up and impressions from the necrogeographic journey laid down in pen and ink. The route taken can be traced in graphite, landmarks assigned and waypoints ticked off. New regions of the urban sprawl chosen for the next drift, and future excursions planned.

The adept should still take care when out and about of course. They will always have more to fear from the living entrenched within their fiercely defended council estates and filthy half shuttered high streets than any of the dead, no matter how belligerent. There may be a reason certain spots on the map boast much higher death rates than others, and neither thin places nor corpse ways need be invoked to explain it.

Dead City Mapping

I have filled many a journal with notes and sketches from my own day long drifts, and even before I knew what psychogeography was I had the innate pull to document what I was seeing and feeling as I let the city take me where it may. Working with actual maps came later, and while they are less personal in their narrative these cartographical tools tend to be far more useful for seeing patterns in the static.

As for the results of all that exploration and research, well it is to allow for the recognition of thin places that the uninitiated would instead ignore. Back when I lived in London I was blessed with an overabundance of such waypoints. Too many to accurately count to be honest, and it is no exaggeration to state that they all began to merge into one another after a while. Still, your mileage, on foot of course, may vary.

Unlike practitioners of more traditional ceremonial magick, or even the classical necromancers of old, modern priests or priestesses of the veil will find themselves to be intimately tied to their local area. This makes sense in hindsight. The death current manifests not only through the minds of those who contemplate the afterlife in any of its thousand forms but also within the landscape itself.

While a map should never be considered the territory, as it is usually out of date from the moment it is printed, such versatile tools do offer a unique crystallisation of the mental perception of space and distance within a handy physical object. Much like a work of fiction it ties together the many loose strands of data that slowly grow around any bounded area, be it inhabited or not.

Thin places, then, are either locations that have seen larger than normal concentrations of murder and decay, or are said to experience regular death current related phenomena such as cyclic hauntings. They can also be areas where the corpse ways meet the material landscape, though actually finding that out may be difficult until a greater familiarity with the local area is gained through regular necrogeographic rituals.

Not ever city will have all of the potential types of waypoints that are tied to the wider discipline of dead city mapping, though even the most modern new town or ancient rural village will have at least a few. These can be collated from a number of sources, be they newspapers, books on true crime, ghost hunting blogs or even long dormant message boards. Word of mouth is worth following up too, though usually with a pinch of salt.

Indeed no potential lead should be ignored, as the opportunity to verify them will likely occur later as the adept is drawn further into the lucid dreams of the wider urban sprawl. The city, much like its dead, can be surprisingly vocal if the adept is willing to stop and listen, and once the spirit of place realises that there is an ear turned in its direction it may focus an impossibly vast and unblinking eye upon the necromancer too.

The adept should pay special attention to locations where the usually relatively uniform coverage of the Veil within the material world has been either lightly damaged or jaggedly pierced. While the barrier between the real and unreal is usually quite robust, a designated place of burial, or a tragic mass loss of life, can create a tear that may never fully heal. These should be added to the necromancer's local map when identified.

Of course the literal souls of the dead do not spill forth from this necrotic gash in the fabric of normality. Such events belong to the realms of fiction, not fact. But the waxing background hum of the death current at those otherwise normal sites can attract ghostforms or wandering souls, astral parasites and poltergeists, mysterious events of all shapes and kinds. Those points of interest too should be noted.

These are the unlucky places, homes that seem to breed multi-generational sickness or hungry lakes that claim numerous victims year after year. Forest clearings where the serial killer hid the bodies, not all of which have been found. Previously undocumented plague pits disturbed by tunnelling work to install mass transit in the suburbs. Overgrown graveyards and ruined church crypts. Maybe the adept's own home.

While generally avoided by the public out of some innate fear of psychic contagion, these less than positive waypoints can provide a stable base camp from which the necromancer is able to experiment within the presence of the wounded Veil. As long as the location allows discreet public access of course.

Legality is an issue that should not be ignored when plotting potential sites for future exploration, however. No matter how heavily the local jail stinks of death, trying to break in and have a look around would be a vary bad idea. The new occupants of the house once owned by a notorious local killer will likely be fed up with teens jumping the back fence to take a peek too. Discretion, as always, is key.

The slowly growing series of circles on the necrogeographic map will begin to form patterns, usually starting from a place of burial outward like a starburst frozen in concrete, and when these are connected those ley lines of the underworld are soon brought to the surface. The corpse ways, paths that the dead walk within the material plane, partly revealed at last.

As a side project places of specifically occult interest can also be noted. The current and former homes of renowned sorcerers. Druidic groves and covensteads. Holy springs and ancient temples to once local gods. Especially storied and long-lived esoteric bookshops are worth remembering, as are the main regional libraries which house some of the original editions of the grimoires that once outlined the necromancer's art.

Practical information, such as hills, forests and trackways can be helpful when on an excursion to find a certain waypoint. Even the route of rivers now repurposed as under street sewers may be of use, the folkloric associations between hidden running water and haunted locations providing an intriguing counterpoint to the usually visual nature of such landmarks.

While these may not directly grant the necromancer a view into the way the death current flows within the wider city, they will gift those explorations a much rounder flavour. Though in the end how the adept chooses to populate their own necrogeographic map is up to them, as long as they remain both honest and clinical in its annotation above all else.

Crossroad Blues

It is always tricky to pin down exactly why something esoteric works the way it does. Even the most skilled magickian is but a child playing with matches, trying not to burn their fingers while lighting the fire. As a result many of the underlying mechanics of the interaction between the seen and unseen worlds remains theoretical, though the insights that I have gleaned over the years do seem to at least fit the evidence.

The idea of corpse ways does still bother me though. While the concept appears to have validity based upon the way they danced like fracture lines throughout my home town, there seem to be far less of them in other places which I have lived over the years. While I doubt they are unique to large cities like London, the questions remains as to why smaller urban areas are not as well covered by those underworld lay lines.

While the corpse ways are an important addition to the adept's understanding of the built space which they inhabit, they seem doubly powerful when they occur near an actual three or four way junction, a liminal point of past and future journeys. The death current waxes strong in such storied locations regardless of other nearby underworld ley lines, allowing for a chance to contact something that is just passing through.

As for why the paths of necromantic significance which the adept notices within the material landscape seem to be so infested by spirits, sites of repeated murders, home to hungry rivers and some very unlucky places, that is a difficult question to answer. Perhaps it is just coincidence, a simple trick of statistics and side effect of the human need to see patterns in the static.

Or maybe the presence of multiple wellsprings of the death current along those invisible lines of human sorrow grant the wandering dead camp grounds of sorts on their eternal hike around the material plane. Hotels and hostelries of the damned, places to refuel and stay until the living within those walls are drained of all useful energy. It is not like they have to worry about how long it takes to arrange dinner, after all.

This may at first seem to be a fanciful position for the accelerated necromancer to take, but there is a raft supporting evidence throughout the folklore of the world. Aside from the wider concept of ley lines as the energetic circulatory system of Gaia, there is also the idea of fairy paths and the ever mobile wild hunt. Neither should be impeded in their journey, on threat of bad luck and perhaps even death.

Almost all esoteric disciplines would also agree that the spirits of the deceased, be they actual departed souls or ghostforms formed from left over mental information, tend to be resistant to efforts to remove them from a given place. What is usually perceived as a previous owner looking to retain dominance of what was once their home may instead simply be an invisible hobo defending its latest meal.

Even if they can be shaken loose, the haunting seems to return within a month or so. Of course, no one thinks to check if it is the same spirit as before, or another etherial vagabond that drifted in to stay a while by the fire and empty the cupboards while doing so. Understandably such questions are rarely as important to the afflicted families as the idea of a good nights sleep. But the uncertainty remains.

Such corpse ways would be doubly significant to the dead if their journey within the material realm is thought of as exploration of a naturally hostile environment. Similar to a still living person who seeks to walk on the bottom of the ocean or within the vacuum of space, the actual state of the surrounding matter would prove detrimental to their continued existence unless a sympathetic technology was employed.

As beings of pure spirit, information, or a heady mix of the two, the ever drifting ghosts which the adept encounters on their journey towards the Veil would be poorly suited to a physical reality in which all actions cost or otherwise burn the very energy they are made up of. This is an innate vitality that those interlopers would be unable to replenish under normal circumstances, lacking as they do a body to generate more.

Any location which seems to have been built upon a wellspring of underworld energy, or that exists on a confirmed necrogeographic waypoint that was generated by a wound in the Veil, will naturally attract those entities who endlessly hunger for the warmth of the living, or desire the cold of the grave. Not all of them are evil, true, but even the ostensibly good ones still need to feed.

And yes, sites of mass burial will definitely be haunted. While folklore states that the dead do not choose to linger around their fleshy remains once they are forced to discard them, that is only half the story. Because the physical decay under the soil and all too human feelings of loss generated by visitors in the cemetery above will attract other ghostly parasites to take up residence instead. Misery loves company, after all.

Junction Opening

We all love a bit of esoteric folklore. Necromancers especially seem to have an eye on the past and respect for those who have gone before. And just like Robert Johnson, said to have sold his soul at a Mississippi crossroads for an almost supernatural mastery of the guitar, there is power in seeking those worldly junctions out. A somewhat lighter touch is required to actually gain from such interactions, though.

If the adept has yet to fully map the corpse ways of their local area, then a back up plan becomes viable. Essentially any three or four way crossroads near a cemetery, or that once held a gallows within it, will also allow for easier contact with the dead. Paths actually inside of the boundaries of the graveyard would be ideal of course, if it was not for too many prying eyes.

Ingredients

Animal bones
Copper coins
Crow feathers
Sulphur
The adept's blood

Optional

Coffin nails
Grave glass

Tools

A glass or earthenware dish
Hand trowel
Thin parchment paper
Three or Four black candles

The point of completing a junction opening is to help attune a certain crossroads to the energetic signature of the adept. Fostering such connections early is generally a good idea, as the necromancer will have use of these thin places later in their practice. While those that are situated near a corpse way are preferred this is not always necessary, but such proximity does make the location easier to initially work with.

Once a quiet spot within general view of the crossroads is chosen, preferably in a ditch, under the cover of some bushes or behind a fence line, the adept sets up the ritual by digging a small hole with the hand trowel. They then press the copper coins, animal bones and sulphur into the earth before using the soil which was previously removed to cover them over. Finally the dish is laid over this buried offering.

Either three or four candles are then set up around its edge, depending upon the actual number of paths that are being opened, in an orientation that roughly mirrors that geographic layout. The crow feathers are laid in centre and a small peace of the parchment paper, preloaded with a number of drops of the necromancer's blood corresponding again to the physical directions of travel, is placed on top.

A summoning call is then intoned, mentioning the underworld deities of choice. While this vocal step is up for personal interpretation, the following example is a good catch all option. When fire is mentioned the adept should light one of the candles, and the whole chant repeated as many times as is necessary to gift flame to them all.

"Dry dirt beneath me, bury me not.

Clear air around me, choke me not.

Glassy water within me, drown me not.

Cleansing fire before me, char me not.

Quiet spirit beside me, judge me not.

Sombre Persephone, avert me not.

Stern Lilith, prevent me not.

Austere Tiamat, impede me not.

Wondering shades, question me not.

Vengeful wraiths, challenge me not.

Whispering crossroads, hamper me not.

Loving Reaper, abandon me not.

Eternal Veil, disavow me not.

This rightful claim, deny me not."

The bloody parchment paper is then torn into strips, the number of which will depend upon the candles used, and one is burned in the flames of each until consumed, in a clockwise motion starting as close to the north as possible. The crow feathers are employed to waft this smoke and aid in its dispersal and placed back in the centre of the dish as each new strip is first introduced to the flames.

The necromancer then waits for a while, sitting watching the flames as the silence begins to ring louder and louder in their ears. Once they are suitably relaxed by this and can hear only the damp thump of their heartbeat it is time to blow out the candles in the opposite order to how they were lit, and pack away the above ground tools in their knapsack before leaving the place to attune for a lunar month.

While the ritual works best new moon to new moon this is not a hard and fast rule. The adept may find that the crossroads still feels resistant to their intent upon subsequent visits. This will become apparent if they still do not see or feel a spiritual presence while performing the death stare operation or otherwise utilising their mediumistic abilities. If this seems to be the case then the ritual may need to be conducted again.

Especially busy thoroughfares are usually difficult to open, due to their high level of mundane footfall, though as mentioned previously proximity to a junction of the corpse ways does help to mitigate that issue. If not, then trial and error may be required to locate a crossroads that will bend to the adept's will.

As for the ingredients, the bone and blood are attractive to the dead, representing as they do their lost physicality and the desire to possess a material form once again. The sulphur is a nod to the underworld and the parchment paper is just a carrier, though if thin enough should burn well. Crow feathers are tied to the scavenging carrion feeder that was once resplendent in them, and certain cthonic goddesses as well.

The candles are representative of the individual paths which make up the crossroads and the copper coins are a payment to the gatekeepers of the underworld to prompt to hear the necromancer's petition. This is not to be perceived as a direct purchase of land but a kind of viewing fee paid to whoever has title to the spiritual spaces that the trackways represent. There is no guarantee they will even listen, much less agree.

Additionally, if the area is especially urban there is a real chance that it will resist the regular form of opening no matter how many times it is applied. In these cases both coffin nails and grave glass can be added to the buried goods to boost the flow of death current within the bounds of the operation. More blood may also be required, though the adept is cautioned against offering too much too soon.

More astute priests and priestesses of the Veil will have also likely noticed that there is no closing of the ritual other than the extinguishing of the candles before packing up and going home, and this is deliberate. The sacred space is designed to linger for the whole lunar month even after the above ground tools are removed, powered by the burned blood and buried bone.

This slowly seeps into, and eventually overwhelms, the energetic signature of the crossroads, granting the adept a kinship with the necrogeographic waypoint and an open junction to use as a staging ground for future interactions with the unseen world. And due to those earlier efforts, far fewer tools will be needed to successfully interact with the wondering spirits while standing betwixt those storied roadways in future.

Chosen Of The Veil

When I was a child I had a wondrous and wild eyed imagination. Never particularly popular among my peers, nor really interested in trying to become so, I retreated into myself and wove stories from the worlds within my mind. Days spent creating one mock medieval empire, years writing and rewriting the history of another. Wars, plagues, famines and golden ages. Knights in tarnished armour wielding bloody steel.

It helped that I was a better than average artist for my age, and soon enough both maps and character sketches would follow in line with those words. The dead which drifted through those East End streets danced upon my inner vision too, some adopted into the narrative, others avoided as the years sluggishly ground my grungy and dyslexic psyche from course coal to razor sharp diamond.

Little did I realise then just how strange my life would one day become, those elaborate daydreams serving me well as I danced among the gravestones decade after decade, never quite alone. In some ways the form that accelerated necromancy takes now, a mix of the spirit of place and ghosts on the wind, has its roots in my literary interests. Though the unreal world I choose to highlight here is anything but fantasy.

Imagined Temples

Accelerated necromancers hold that while the Veil is seen as a gateway to the otherworld, it is in many ways just a metaphor for the divide between the material and immaterial realms. Mental shorthand as opposed to a definite geographic location, the term is used to describe the murky water that keeps the living and the dead from seeing each other, and the mirrored glass which stops them from touching once again.

As a barrier it overlays the entirety of existence, flowing through the very atoms that define solid, liquid and gas. A silvery black skin which oozes from every wall, pools in the streets. Quicksand of the waking mind and soporific to the souls of those who have gone before. Each breath draws that sickly miasma into the body, marking another grain of sand falling through the hourglass held in the gentle grip of the Reaper.

As the living see the world so the dead do too, though perhaps the latter would struggle to comprehend the changes which have occurred while they lay in cold storage within the confines of Tiamat's womb. Not that many possess either the energy or desire to return anyway, and as a result the necromancer is more likely to encounter wandering spirits, or lingering ghostforms if that paradigm is preferred, on this side of the Veil.

Creatures of ritual, humanity in general has always needed a place to pray. It is through this innate desire to find solace in the arms of the divine that entire religions have spurred their adherents to commit the most heinous acts, all in an effort to gain ground in foreign lands. Churches and temples usually follow shortly after, each a tattoo of godly ownership etched into the disputed flesh of Gaia herself.

Yet when it is realised that the Veil is everywhere the very idea of such immobile monuments to the deities who govern the workings of the otherworld will also seem to lose its appeal. Thin places exist, of course. And spirits are easier to encounter at certain locations. The tendrils of the death current may permeate all things, but it waxes stronger where burials or murders have occurred. Those wounds fester still.

Like the hermits of old the adept should strive to carry their temples with them wherever they go. Internalised cathedrals hewn from bone and blood, once enough practice is gained these arterial monoliths are able to be erected in a moment within the lens of the minds eye. Sanctuary internalised and ready to use with a minimum of fuss. Visualisation proving itself once again to be a keystone of the necromancer's art.

How easy it is to cement this crypt within the psyche will depend upon the skill and concentration of the adept, though. There are few among even the uninitiated who lack the ability to visualise and imagine, to wonder freely through lucid dreams while very much awake. The only real issue will be one of time, as some will inevitably struggle more than others during the installation of this necessarily liminal mental space.

The first shape that the adept should try and see before them is the tunnel. Analogous to their spine, this dungeon like corridor has solid bone walls, a white marbled floor and high vaulted ceilings. Individual vertebrae are represented in the regular ridges which twist and grate against each other as the construct attempts to retain it's form, giving the whole construction a suitably organic feel.

Once the necromancer can visualise themselves walking from one end of this space to the other in first person, and hold that concept in their minds eye for many minutes at a time, then the ritual rooms can be added. Each of these is an arched rib extending from openings at the sides of the vertebrae corridor, and the contents takes the form that is most required during their every day practice.

A library to aid with memory recall perhaps, each book annotated with facts and trivia that may otherwise be forgotten. Or a circular scrying chamber with an impossibly large and perfectly spherical boulder of the most reflective obsidian designed to gift the adept with an insight into both worlds at once. A bank of computers that allow dial up access to the akashic records. A protective circle of razor sharp rock salt.

Spaces to calm the mind can be moulded out of shards of bone, hot springs bubbling with enervating blood set to leach away the aches caused by a particularly difficult series of real world rituals. Darkened coffin lined side rooms to aid in sleep and the prevention of nightmares. Galleries of symbols created along marrow lined pillars, each a sigil promoting a preprogrammed response during trying times.

The options are as endless as the adept is inventive. For those who excel at creating servitors these can be internalised as a temple staff of sorts, similar to the role played by neophytes of old, bringing the thrum of not quite life to the otherwise sterile internal space that the necromancer created. Defensive constructs can be placed in nerve lined barracks, sleeping soundly until a threat is encountered and the warning bell sounds.

And once enough familiarity is gained that visualising the walk along those spinal catacombs becomes second nature then the actual main hall of this imagined temple can finally be constructed. Representing the skull of the adept, herein they may make contact with their personality in its many aspects, to prod and poke at the parts of themselves that they find uncomfortable. A perfect place to safely conduct shadow work.

Here too can they lay the alters to their gods and goddesses, bringing a little of what initially drew them towards the veneration of that particular deity to dwell within their own psyche as well. Boons are far easier to receive when the entity that is granting them has a direct method of delivery to the recipient, and letting a shard of that spirit coexist within the psyche is a handy way to skip the queue.

In a universe that is moulded from information clothed in a veneer of physicality there need not be any real difference between the contents of the necromancer's head and the world that surrounds it. Hubris perhaps and solipsism for definite, but regardless of such closed minded admonitions creating an imagined temple can and will aid in the learning that is to come as the slow walk along the cemetery path continues.

Grief And Loss

Everything ends. Relationships fall by the wayside, friendships fade. And once the book closes on the final chapter of our lives, those who we leave behind can only wonder about the conversations left unsaid. Somehow making it into middle age I have seen far too many of those around me laid into the soil, and despite my more esoteric leanings the loss still bites down just as hard every time.

That said it is our role as priests or priestesses of the Veil to try and bring some solace to those experiencing a similar pain when asked to do so. This must always be as a result of deliberate requests only of course. The balance is not served by lunging forward to colonise the private sorrow of others. In the end the accelerated necromancer cannot claim to have all the answers. Experience, though, is another matter.

Humanity is cursed with a deep knowledge of their state as finite, mortal beings. This pull to the grave manifests in different ways depending upon the personality type of the individual. Some seek dangerous hobbies, challenging the Reaper to take them early. Others stay safely by the sidelines, hoping to make it through another year without incident. But the majority would rather ignore the topic entirely.

Time and again good people are taken from the world, forced to make that final journey beyond the Veil. Evil despots, dictators and murderers too of course, though they are rarely mourned and for good reason. In between are the morally grey among the social group, by far the biggest single catch-all category, and the kind of people who scramble for solace as their loved ones slip away.

Because no matter how emotionally cold the individual watching those strained final breaths may be, each passing is still a stark reminder that all must eventually be called to the Otherworld. Saint, sinner, kings or paupers, the grave will take them all. This is the true fate of all living things, and barring some cataclysmic event which ends recorded history overnight there will always be a need to make sense of the pain.

It falls to the necromancer, poised upon the liminal space between the material and the unseen like an ancient raven, to help those who seek their aid in the difficult task of metabolising those deeply personal yet globally recognised emotions. But this is also an inherently dangerous task, especially when those offering the assistance have no formal training in grief counselling or its allied disciplines.

If in doubt the adept should always leave this area of the art to the professionals. The potential to cause lasting harm, as well as burn the fragile emotional bridges connecting close friends or birth family together through poorly chosen words, is too great to ignore. No, everything is not going to be alright. And yes, the person on the receiving end of such dubious advice has every right to hate the person offering it to them.

The psychedelic whirlpool of emotions fighting for control within the psyche of the uninitiated can be considered dangerous even as they tiptoe through the best day of their life. Alternatively, on a bad one this rage and frustration inherent to the human condition is amplified a thousandfold, and may well see expression through words and fists.

The weeks following the passing of a deeply cherished friend or family member will push this internal dial further towards chaos, the normal balance of their responses to outside stimuli manifesting through a net of conflicting memories and subtle mental triggers. Again, if the priest or priestess of the veil is inexperienced in dealing with such matters then it is best to leave well alone.

Here the morals of those who are more focussed upon the mediumistic aspects of the art are brought into question. If the necromancer is regularly involved in séances or Ouija based board meetings then such conversations with both the not quite gone and perhaps better off forgotten will be a regular part of their day to day work. And when offering those services to the bereaved for money, a conflict of interest is likely.

No adept should feel obliged to deny their gifts in an arena that makes it safe to show them off without fear of religious or societal reprisal. The priest or priestess of the Veil needs to eat like anyone else, and no matter how lucky they are at finding exactly what they need the electricity bill cannot be paid by sheer willpower alone. The books on fake forgotten lore required to keep up with everyone else do not grow on trees, either.

But to venture onto that already shaky moral ground for profit may not be the best way to honour the Reaper, and that choice is one that the medium must make on their own. Regardless of material necessity or spiritual motivation, a background knowledge of how the human psyche bends and eventually breaks under the weight of loss is recommended ahead of time. Personal experience can help, but training is key to success.

Grief counselling is a finely tuned art, and also one best left to strangers, as many of the thoughts and feelings that are bubbling like lava beneath the surface would be better discussed outside of the usual family or friendship group. Yet if the necromancer does want to help, then a specifically hands off and usually pretty quiet methodology can prove useful, but only with the consent of the bereaved.

In fact, common courtesy dictates that the accelerated adept should at least offer an understanding ear for those who are so mired in grief that even just a chance to vent those pent up emotions may help. This is not an excuse to allow the weight of others to sink the likely already precarious ship that the necromancer sails through the cultural waterways, however. Magickian, heal thyself is the golden rule here.

Because if also dealing with their own grief they have every right to put themselves first, though an intriguing quirk of the art seems to be a natural attraction to the emotional distress of others, specifically with relation to the loss of loved ones or group tragedy. Another reason why those who walk the cemetery path are considered by some to be ghouls, and not the necrophagic kind.

Perhaps the adept finds value in those cases because it helps them to work through their own feelings, or maybe it is the cold kiss of the death current between the tears which attracts them instead. Either way, allowing a caring side to leak through their otherwise cold countenance can win friends in unlikely places, as well as allow for a greater understanding of the role that grief plays in prioritising the good things in life.

The priest or priestess of the Veil must always remember that the pain is not theirs to revel in, however, nor do they get a say in how it is dealt with unless they are specifically skilled in such seemingly arcane psychological arts. They are a companion on the journey, but the direction of travel does not automatically grant them any right to push others towards a certain understanding or outcome.

Ultimately just being there is the best method for healing those who are unable to work their way through the complexities of either their mortality or that of family and friends. Taking a colleague out for a coffee and letting them share as little or as much as they like can soothe even the most broken of hearts. Should they prefer to keep that pain private then just changing the topic and carrying on as normal works wonders too.

In Funerary Wake

I will never understand the fear in some people's voices when speaking about the dead. Yes, there are some health concerns when decomposition sets in, and the resulting changes are far from pleasant to look at. But to deny the necessary role of death in the realm of the living is to divorce yourself from so much of that rich, sometimes uncomfortable context.

And that means I handle the funerary rituals of my culture a little differently, spinning a celebratory narrative around otherwise tragic events, one which is also subtly laced with a classical call to the dead. I feel that there is no shame in such frivolity when facing the graveside. I am not here to insult the memory of those who were once loved, but to honour them like they deserve instead.

Funerals need not be sad affairs. Reverent, of course, but to focus exclusively on the loss that the mourners are feeling cheapens the memory of those who are now sadly gone. The adept is uniquely suited to these melodramatic rites of passage, and with a little forward planning even the dullest of gatherings can be balanced after the fact with a show of solidarity for the role that body will go on to play in the green world.

But few who walk the cemetery path alongside the ever understanding Reaper are public about their esoteric interests, and many find it safer to toil under a mainstream religious veneer. The accelerated necromancer is honour bound to attend the laying of a friend, regardless of the objectionable location chosen or litanies sung to the gods of the Abrahamic pantheon.

Because should the deceased or their executors be looking for a conventional burial then it is likely that the actual service will be conducted in the prevailing style for that region. Usually within some form of grand chapel or side building, and in the case of either agnostics or Neopagans the clerical ministrations tend to retain a somewhat muted Christian tone by default.

It is not the place of the adept to force others who seek such bland reassurance from their chosen spirituality to see the truth of the unreal world. Each to their own. But the more enforced solemnity of those mainstream observances will put the adept in a position where they must at least play lip service to the idea that the dead are objects of misery for the living when surrounded on all sides by the uninitiated.

Respect for the actions of the Reaper can be displayed through other, more focussed means though. As long as some of those who are bearing otherwise wilting witness to that passing are on board with taking part in a slightly more unconventional wake after the priest has gone back to counting the contents of the collection plate, then the necromancer is more than equipped to quite literally set the menu.

Celebration and revelry in times of tragedy need not be disrespectful. The uninitiated fail to recognise that the dead are actually empowered by their coming transformation, transmuted into overripe seeds planted in the freshly tilled soil. Laid beneath the earth they transcend the mortal limitations that once pinned that body like a grounded butterfly to the canvas of space and time.

Death remains a necessary process. Every journey must come to an end to have any direction in the first place. Free from pain and their own heart-ache at loves lost, those who become one with the womb of Tiamat are blessed with an end to suffering and yet also cursed to transfer that pain to those left behind. This is the weight that all carry in their final moments, though few have the presence of mind to realise that fact.

Existing in a deliberate blind spot created by the uninitiated to shelter those who still draw breath from having to think about a time when they will no longer do so, people who once basked in the love and adoration of family closest to them become an eldritch and unwanted monster best ignored. Folklore tells tales of such beings. Morality as fact and a heavy dose of admonition for supposed sins along the way too.

The real vampires are not nocturnal lovers or tortured heroes, though. They dwell as metaphors in the minds of friends and family, returning unbidden as the reverberations of their life continue to roll around the spaces where they once lived. And oh, how those unreal spectres nibble away at the vitality of their captive audience, reminding them of their mortality through floods of great sobbing tears.

Decomposition is fascinating. Dwelling in an unseen subterranean space where the workings of decay happen out of sight and rarely brought to mind, each body is a wondrously silent catalyst of future change. There the newly interred lay in that darkness, slowly leeching nutrients into the very earth itself while universes of bacteria ripple into existence and burn out just as quickly inside them.

The skulls of the dead grin wide in their chrysalises of wood and metal, for they know what wonders will one day grow in their biological shadow. Evolution that they will never witness, yet could not occur without the meat to feed it. This harsh truth of decay is a foundational tenet of the death current in the Western world. It is also the primal honesty that the accelerated necromancer chooses to share.

When the adept is called to lead a funerary rite they must strike a balance between sadness for the life taken and joy for that which will one day come from those obfuscated, yet vital, remains. This is a fine line to walk, for the opportunity to say the wrong thing around those who know not the wonders of the cemetery path is an ever present problem. So perhaps the answer, then, is not to speak at all.

The idea of holding a dumb supper in honour of those who have travelled to the Otherworld has admittedly disputed origins. Though attempts have been made to provide sources which will tie the practice to a longstanding necromantic or mediumistic through line, the tradition seems to be a relatively modern mutation of a divinatory practice that hailed from rural America during the early days of the 20th Century.

Starting in the Ozark and Appalachian areas of the United States, but spreading relatively widely among the Irish and Scottish immigrants who made that land their new home, the ritual was originally a way to conjure up the still living soul of a future husband to be. In this way it was almost exclusively performed by unmarried women in a spirit of daring challenge not unlike modern legend tripping.

The exact point where this narrative switched to one of ancestral veneration is impossible to know, but perhaps the liminal nights chosen for such events, such as Halloween, would cause a merging of those otherwise opposed mythological currents. Regardless, by the dawn of the new Millennium the term almost exclusively referred to the more necromantic version of the rite when mentioned in the media.

Of course people pass away all year round, so while the overt death current driven nature of that late autumn holiday is useful for general rites, dumb suppers do not only work around that time. And for the reverent celebration of the recently interred, be it the height of summer or darkest winter, they are an observation that holds a rare charm.

The evening starts with the choice of food. While classical necromancers would drink only brackish water before eating undercooked dog flesh and burnt toast to commune more closely with the spirit realm, the modern version has lost the desire for subtle self poisoning. As such a standard three or four course set up is recommended, and because these will be served in reverse the desert or cheese platter will be up first.

The focus should be on foods that the person who passed away enjoyed in life. Not only does this acknowledge an understanding of their culinary interests, but also adds a small nod to postmortem cannibalism, albeit without the human carrion or risk of brain dissolving disease. Mimicking their diet for a meal so soon after their passing is the next best thing to call them back to the table to join in.

The most important aspect of a dumb supper is the lack of conversation.

From the moment the necromancer calls the meal to order, usually with a short statement about the rules of the game and to remind everyone whose memory the gathering is being called to honour, no one must say a word. Sighs, sobs or coughs should all be restricted to involuntary actions only, and of course laughter is kept until the end.

Optionally, the vision of those in attendance can also be obscured and cotton wool or earplugs used to deaden sound as well. This will require a little more work from the adept however, as they will need to both make any food easy enough to eat while unable to see and also gently tap all those at the table on the shoulder once the next course is served.

The meal continues in both reversed order and reverent silence until a special final starter of nuts and seeds is brought before the diners, a strident symbol of the rebirth that the body now cocooned beneath the soil will one day promote. Any allergies should be planned for ahead of time, though, and this step skipped for those who have them. At this point restraints on vision and hearing are removed so conversation can begin.

It is recommended to use this time to relate humorous or heart-warming tales of the deceased, and laugh heartily but also honestly as they are shared. The night ends with a ritualised giving of paper invitations to the meal that was previously consumed at the door while the guests leave, serving as a memento of the ritual that everyone took part in and also a tactile expression of the event's reversed nature.

The final act that the accelerated necromancer undertakes is one of cleaning up the leftovers. These are placed in a food safe Tupperware or ziplock bag and left out for scavengers or birds somewhere that the deceased would have recognised while alive. They can also be left on the grave itself, though may draw some confused looks from the cemetery workers should the choice be made to do so.

Physical Factors

While some may perceive the following topics as needlessly negative, respecting the balance requires that the accelerated adept actually faces the darker side of the art. That said many of the areas that will be lightly brushed upon here are not initially considered to be of necromantic origin, at least in the sense of appearing within the pages of dusty grimoires or initiatory school syllabuses.

But just as death is a constant in the human realm so the many rotten veins that lead to the development of that esoteric discipline should be explored. This is especially true of the various ways which the living have treated the remains of the dead over the centuries. History, much like misery, loves company. And as a result my travels took me to many a museum seeking to converse with those who were trapped there under glass.

I have heard those otherwise silent historical echoes calling from the cases that now house their mortal remains, marvelled at the funerary incantations which are etched into the sarcophagi and wept when witnessing a fate worse than death itself. Because to be put on display in such a way, gawked at by school children and disinterested teachers alike, is just desecration disguised as science and nothing more.

Grave Desecrations

Regardless of how far the adept has come along their cemetery path it is inevitable that they will spend at least a little of their life around the bodies of the deceased. Whether conducting a dumb supper after the funeral rites of a friend, or holding the hand of a loved one a little too tightly after they have already slipped away, showing all due respect to the material shell is in many ways a forgotten cornerstone of the wider art.

Indeed there are those on the fringes of the more classical form of necromancy who see the body as little better than a storehouse of ritualistic tools to be manipulated as they see fit. Cut, probed, dried and ground to dust at a whim. Skulls stolen and flesh displayed. Burial clothes as ritual robes. Ashes for drawing circles. Desecration by those destined to lay on a similar slab while hoping for more human decency.

It goes without saying that these acts are a deep insult to both the balance and the deities of the Veil. While the accelerated adept has no need for poetic rhymes to remember their morality, nor a belief in threefold return to browbeat them into some form of fear induced positivity, they do tend to want to do the right thing for its own sake. The seven necromantic laws neatly highlight this altruistic train of thought.

The history associated with mistreating the bodies of the dead goes back to a time long before the grimoire tradition and its laundry list of bizarre spell ingredients took Western esotericism hostage. What little is known about the earliest burials, mostly situated within the Middle East and undertaken during the Palaeolithic era, shows an enigmatic but growing respect for human remains later generations would forget.

While corpse disposal likely started as a way to deter scavengers and stop the spread of disease within the communal living space, these practical considerations hardly address the shift towards the solemn laying of friends and family in the earth surrounded by tools and trinkets, animals and even the odd stillborn child. Which underworld gods were called upon for safe travel, if any, will likely never be known either.

Yet not every cadaver interred was placed there willingly. As can be seen with the ongoing research into the almost immaculately preserved Iron Age bog bodies which have been found littered around Northern Europe, it is safe to say that sacrifices too were readily offered to the spirits of soil and stream. As the seeds lay dormant below the ground so did the spirits who governed their growth, and those forces had to be fed.

This would not count as desecration if the victim were breathing their last as the marshy ground took them, true, but based on the lack of water residue in many of their lungs this was not always the case. A number of examples are now thought to have been members of the social group marked out through birth defects or by a drawing of lots before being killed, their bodies bartered to the underworld for any number of reasons.

Some of the more heavily wounded specimens are assumed to be the few badly beaten survivors of inter clan warfare, given to the gods of the land as an offering for future victories upon it. A romanticised way of looking at such leathery artifacts of a truly pagan pre-Roman Europe perhaps, but while cultures develop at an alarming rate in the modern era a little shard of that need to show mastery over the dead still remains.

Always a warlike species, the sheer amount of otherwise good and healthy people denied the proper burial rites while being left to lay where they fell is staggering. But simply paying no heed to the corpses that are piling up in the plains and mountains as a hulking war machine rolls through that territory is not directly an act of desecration. No, that would entail the deliberate and perhaps public destruction of the body itself.

The idea of being hung, drawn and then quartered is a mainstay of English history and was codified into law as a punishment for treason in the 14th century. Yet in reality this was a far more brutal process than the title first appears. After being dragged by horse to the place of execution the victim was hung until almost dead. The genitals and entrails would then be removed to be burned before the delirious eyes of the criminal.

An all too merciful beheading soon followed, and the body would then be carved into rough quarters with the different sections being sent to notable locations around the nation to quash further dissent. While the baying crowds were permitted to witness the bloody emasculation of male traitors, females accused of treason were burned at the stake to protect the public decency instead. A truly strange distinction indeed.

The severed body parts of enemy combatants displayed as warnings or made into trophies is a surprisingly common tactic, running in a through line from the dawn of civilisation right up to the modern era. That said times have changed. So less gory acts of corpse destruction, usually based around some religious taboo as opposed to literal heads on spikes, prevail upon the laser guided battlefields of the 21st Century.

Of course military desecration is a separate issue to those that are carried out by civilians or state run institutions, and murky water for the necromancer to try and swim within for sure. While these excesses are abhorrent, unless the adept is also a serving member of the armed forces then little can be done to change those attitudes outside of hoisting the perpetrators before the court of public opinion to pay the price.

During the heyday of the Roman empire the punishments for certain especially serious crimes, including treason, was to be strangled and then mutilated post mortem before being left on the Gemonian Stairs in full view of the senate. The bodies of especially reviled criminals were brought to the city from all over the empire to share in that grisly fate, alongside a number of senators and even Emperor Vitellius himself.

Starting in the 11th Century the field of medieval medicine would fall afoul of a simple mistranslation that ultimately caused the desecration of embalmed Egyptian remains on an industrial scale. The similarity of the term mumia, which describes a very specific tarry bitumen prised by the Persians for treating minor wounds, and the word mummy led to the latter being collected so sarcophagi resins could be harvested.

In time the practice would evolve further, and the entire body would be offered up to the proto-pharmacist's blade. At one point the demand was so high that the freshly dead were dried and embalmed just so they could be sold on again as a cure for everything from cancer to an upset stomach. Wrappings were ground to powder and taken with alcohol, a dose of purest snakeoil if ever there was one.

Unbelievably the dried flesh of those once respectfully sleeping cadavers would also be widely used as a pigment that swirled dark brown strokes of paint on canvasses from the 16th to 19th Centuries too. And wealthy Victorians, upon hearing tales of sandy deserts and forgotten pharaonic empires, began holding unwrapping parties, where mummies were needlessly divested of their last strips of dignity.

Medical cannibalism is not restricted to the West. The Mellified Man was a legendary Arabian substance created by steeping a corpse in honey for a hundred or so years until it began to liquefy, and then eventually become partly mummified as well. Once potted this likely foul tasting confection was said to be blessed with astonishing healing properties. Regardless, it commanded a high price in the markets where it was sold.

Chinese sources, reporting on this practice, would elaborate further. Here the men who offered themselves up for such a gooey fate were thought to be both elderly and have no means of supporting themselves in their old age, so had very little to lose by indulging their sweet tooth one last time at the pharmacists expense. And yes, this particular concoction was likely just pure honey with a mystical back story to drum up trade.

Human fat was definitely considered to be useful in a variety of medicinal scenarios though. Surprisingly its topical use saw widespread adoption across Europe and executioners even turned a profit selling the *Axungia hominis* of their state sanctioned victims to the public. It seems that Paracelsus, the 16th Century physician, had a hand in codifying this trend even if it predated his teachings by many hundreds of years.

A similar nod can be given to the Parisian butchers who offered purported *graisse de guillotiné* during the French Revolution as well. The hand of glory, perhaps most famous of all execution related ritual tools, also saw its heyday in England around this time. Well known in rural folklore as being able to put an entire house to sleep when burned, it was implicated in a number of burglaries and non-violent crimes.

This grim necromantic staple relied upon the desecration of at least two corpses to create. The fat from an executed criminal was formed into a candle which was later placed in the death grip of another gibbeted felon, after their left hand was removed at the wrist and dried. Various other ingredients were listed during this pickling process, including salt, urine, vervain and horse dung, though that last addition is disputed.

While the hand of glory may seem to be a fanciful slice of European folklore corpse dismemberment for esoteric purposes has endured well into the 21st Century. Be it inexperienced sorcerers opening graves to harvest materials or coffins dragged into the sunlight before their inhabitants are staked during some ham-fisted attempt at vampire slaying, those who sleep beneath the soil are rarely as safe as they should be.

Of course the accelerated necromancer, while happy to turn a bloodshot eye towards such historical curios, will find no value in the desecration of human remains for its own sake. More focussed on the manipulation of life force and the social aspects of death as a psychic contagion within the modern mind, they consider their position as priests and priestesses of the Veil to be a sacred, and above all else reverent, custodianship.

Rotting Away

Unlike other necromancers I am not in the habit of handling physical remains. Yes, there have been times when I have had no other choice but to be around corpses in various states of decay, though I try to keep these to a minimum out of a mix of dutiful respect for the deceased and general dislike for rotten, necrotic flesh. Animal bones are always a welcome addition to my knapsack though, if properly cleaned.

It was an aversion to the quickly building whirlwind of bacterial forces within the body that led me to approach necromancy from a more cultural and memetic angle in the first place, to find a way to work within the death current without having to be around those at times very rancid decompositional materials. And I think I succeeded, though it took a storied detour into the non-tradition of chaos magick to do so.

While most people would likely prefer to ignore the eventual fate of the physical shell post mortem the adept does not have that luxury. Ignorance breeds incorrect ideas about the nature of death and decay, as well as romanticising what is in some places a very disgusting process best viewed from a distance. Indeed those fringe necromantic paths that regularly handle putrescent remains are playing a very dangerous game.

Plus the actual mechanics of the dissolution process, while never beautiful, do hold a certain morbid charm on a purely technical level, allowing as they do for the relatively quick clean up of biological matter and the return of much needed nutrients to the soil. Efforts to forestall this process, such as embalming, also display human ingenuity in the face of the inevitable. Futile actions, true, but worthy of note.

Of course the stages of decay are not set in stone, and there are a number of biological or environmental factors to consider when discussing such obviously arbitrary timescales. Body mass for one, as well as the position of the remains with regards to easy access for the insects that would usually be attracted to them. Temperature, humidity, missing limbs and open wounds. All of these can also alter the following plan.

One: Freshly Deceased

Running from roughly five minutes post death to around three days afterwards, the initial stage in the afterlife cycle is typified by rigor mortis. This locks the muscles in place from around hours four to twelve, though this can vary. The eyes become cloudy and livor mortis occurs as the blood in the circulatory system pools at the lowest point, causing a dull red discolouration of the skin.

Inside a storm of activity has begun as the bacterial contents of the intestines and those once held at bay within the walls of individual cells begin to break the body down from the inside out. Internal organs liquefy and this attracts flying insects to any wound or other opening where they lay their eggs. These usually hatch within the first 24 hours and the larvae start to aid in the deconstruction effort.

Two: Postmortem Bloating

This stage begins around four days after death. As the bacteria continue to dissolve cells and break down the soft tissues there is a marked increase in insect swarming as gases including methane, cadaverine, hydrogen sulphide and putrescine attract them. Those foul smelling compounds build up during this process and bloat the body before escaping, causing a release of foamy blood from mouth and nose as they do so.

Proper embalming, which is usually undertaken within the first day or so, will stop the decomposition from advancing to this stage while awaiting burial. By removing the liquids and bacteria from the body cavity as well as draining the circulatory system of any remaining contents swelling is relegated to the stomach area and significantly reduced overall. There is also less surface discolouration outside of livor mortis too.

Three: Active Decay

Ten days or so after death the decay within the body cavity reaches critical mass and due to cellular damage the skin is unable to prevent those internalised gases from being released. As it does so the body deflates, helped by the rupturing of the outer surface and draining of remaining fluids into the surrounding environment. The skin slips and colonies of insects are now visible in the muscles and fats underneath.

There is also a marked rise in temperature as bacteria continue breaking down the remaining tissues. The older maggots will abandon the body at this stage and retreat to softer ground to pupate. Beetles and wasps will begin a predatory role as well as laying their eggs within the quickly blackening husk. The smell is extremely unpleasant, and will remain so until both the deflated remains and surrounding area dries.

Four: Advanced Decay

This second to last stage of the afterlife cycle begins some twenty days after death and represents the end of large scale bacterial activity. With the almost total removal or liquefaction of the soft tissues that supported the smaller insects the focus instead shifts towards larger beetles and cheese flies who are capable of chewing through what little flesh remains.

The smell has reduced in potency as the body begins to ferment, and any parts that are in contact with the surrounding environment will grow mould. Rapidly drying, what was once a living and vibrant creature is now little better than a jumbled collection of blackened connective tissue surrounding bones scattered by the actions of insect larvae and fluid dispersal.

Five: Skeletal remains

This occurs any time from fifty or so days after death, and the exact date will depend upon a number of environmental factors as well as insect actions. The body and surrounding surfaces are now completely dry and the smell is almost gone. Any hair that remains will attract certain types of moth whose larvae feed on this otherwise hardy material.

Bones bleach over time when left to the elements and due to dispersal by larger animals can be found many miles from the original site of decomposition. They also disintegrate relatively rapidly in excessively warm and damp locations as bacteria return to consume the collagen that holds them together. The calcium phosphate which makes up their other main ingredient also dissolves in acidic, peaty soil.

Bloodwork

I have been conducting blood sorcery rituals for almost as long as I have considered myself a magickian. Something about the taboo nature of such reasoned self mutilation along with the inherent power that seems to echo within those crimson droplets has always fascinated me.

But have a care, fellow adept, for moderation is key and there is no bene-fit in self harm for its own sake. Many an explorer into the physical has lost themselves to the pleasures of the flesh and fallen from the lofty goals they once set themselves, either magickal or mundane. But I am sure you can do better.

Blood. More so than even skin or bone, it is the very oxygen rich plasma coursing through the necromancer's veins which defines their status as a functioning expression of the ghost in that machine. No matter the horrific damage to the musculoskeletal system, organs or nerves, as long as that crimson fluid still circulates freely then life in the purely mechanistic sense remains intact.

Not just a physical shell, the body itself forms a unique expression of the DNA which from conception holds the template for what the creature will one day become. It could be argued that, at least in this incarnation at least, those swirling strands of nucleotides are the adept's true magickal name.

And as with the sages of old, to know the name of a thing is to be granted power over it. Or in this case, to work with the adept's own DNA is to put a little of themselves in everything they do.

While horror films and genre fiction have tried to assert that blood can be consumed to drain the life force from within, this is untrue. There are too many health risks to condone such actions, and the necromancer would do better to look elsewhere for a free meal.

Pathogens and bloodbourne diseases can be ingested through drinking that warm arterial fluid, be it human or animal, leading to a high risk of possible infection. While the digestive system regularly dissolves many of the bacteria which enter the body through the mouth, it does not provide a guaranteed defence.

So while hematophagy as a lifestyle may seem enticing for the more transgressively minded adept, in truth any more than a little taste here and there can be deadly. This is not an exaggeration. A regular intake of blood large enough to provide real nutritional value among adepts would actually be life threatening due to one of its main constituents. Iron.

Unlike bats and leeches the human digestive system did not develop to filter out such a large intake of ferrous metals. Not only ulceration of the stomach lining but eventual organ failure, coma and death will occur unless the practice is conducted in strict moderation.

Transfusions and ingestion are very different processes, and while the former is a medically accepted method for assisting those with a genuine need the latter has proven to have no such benefits outside of perhaps feeding a purely psychological desire among the various communities that have clotted around the idea of crimson immortality.

But while drinking blood may be off the table due to health concerns, there are many ways it can be utilised in a ritualistic context without ever needing to pass the lips. By far the simplest is when drawing or firing sigils, because the obviously pictographic nature of those condensations of magickal desire lend themselves well to a little hematographical penmanship.

Extraction is best undertaken with a brand new medical lancet, as these are deliberately designed to provide a clean wound, and the press to fire type can be operated one handed. Scalpels and push pins are acceptable, though must be disinfected and thoroughly dry before use to avoid the risk of contamination.

If a bladed implement is chosen then the adept must remember that what they have seen in movies and on television is pure fantasy. There is no need to fully slash the palm, nor should any body part other than the fingers be cut to produce the blood flow required for ritual. A pin prick here, a scalpel pressed into the pad of the thumb there, but only a drop or two is more than enough.

No matter which method is chosen the necromancer must have medical supplies ready should they accidentally gouge instead of poke. And it goes without saying that anyone who suffers from issues with clotting or has any form of immune deficiency should avoid working in this medium at all for the sake of personal safety.

On its own blood is a poor drawing medium unless treated properly. It will coagulate and harden relatively quickly outside of the human body, though a little acidic base such as lemon juice can hold that at bay for a while. This can then be mixed in with the ink of choice and either pulled up into a fountain pen via the piston or used with a brush as needed.

This blended liquid may rot unless refrigerated or frozen and a fresh few drops taken when a new project is being started is the safest option. When applied to either paper or parchment it will dry a rusty brown that is mostly indistinguishable from any other type of consecrated ink.

A store bought base liquid of a similar colour is actually acceptable in this case, as the energy will be derived from the blood and not the medium it is being carried within during the drawing process. Many such magickal inks are available, though the necromancer need not acquire anything as intricate or expense as that to generate viable results.

Of course the adept will know the weight that DNA adds to the mix, and the inherent power in placing their true magickal name within the lines. It goes without saying that this should never be done lightly or for others, as it directly ties the very spirit of the original donor to the outcome.

Yes, acts of dominion can be conducted by writing letters to the chosen target using this blend, imposing the necromancer's will through contact with their blood, though it is highly discouraged to do so. Not only does such an operation fly in the face of the victim's own autonomy, but there are more mundane concerns such as communicable diseases or leaving actual incriminating evidence on the page to worry about.

Far safer is the concept of the dead letter, a request written in blood infused words and then mailed to a non-existent address. These will eventually find a final home in the undeliverable box at the local postal warehouse, where they can remain indefinitely, out of sight and out of mind.

Once the lost letter has been held for a while it may well be destroyed, incinerated so as to keep the information inside secure. And thus it is freed to the winds of fate, a sigil charged by every hand the envelope passed through to get there. Yes, this is indeed low magick as a crowd funded sorcery of sorts, and all for the price of a second class stamp.

As a final note, all supplies used during both the creation and expression of these extremely personal inks will need to be thoroughly cleaned with hot water after use, to prevent the build up of mould or other biological material where the blended ink had been. Blades disinfected and Lancets disposed of as per the instructions given on the packet. Better safe than sick, as they say.

Blood has many other uses outside of graphic design or dead letters, of course. In its original state, such as when squeezed from a small cut on the finger tip, it can be used in candle dressings or offering dishes designated for the necromancer's deity of choice.

Not only is this empowering from a ritualistic point of view, containing as it does a tiny spark of the adept's own life force, but along with tears and spittle will attract those pseudo-spirits who yearn for the flesh they once knew. Moderation is key here too, as the adept should be wary of any god or goddess which demands regular blood sacrifice, or threatens consequences when these are not provided.

It will also instantly set the atmosphere of a ritual chamber when a drop or two is added to the charcoal disks before the chosen dry blend incense, encoding the very air itself with the necromancer's essence and therefore their magickal will as well. Blood on the fingertips when pinching out the candles at the end of a given operation will also underline the fact that what is done is now and irreversibly complete.

Returning to offering bowls, flint and obsidian remember the untold gallons of both human and animal blood that they have spilled over the centuries, while copper and iron also resonate with the desire to slake their thirst on that warm arterial liquid as well.

Any blade which has taken a human life in combat will also call to the necromancer. The desire to be free to do so again expressed through mental images associated with their perhaps gory history when the priest or priestess of the Veil is standing close to them, though these sometimes vengeful wraiths are best left in the museum display cases where they can do no more harm.

Considering just how deeply the adept's very existence depends on the blood circulating through their mortal frame is it unsurprising that it plays such an important part in their sorcery. Those who would seek to become more than just a ghost in the machine are right to treat it with such reverence, because their true name is never expressed as well anywhere else.

Becoming The Bulwark

I have always lived in haunted houses of one kind or another. Some of those early homes, council owned and endlessly reassigned to broken families surviving lives of quiet desperation in the inherently materialistic underclasses of both Thatcherite and then Blairite Britain may not have had bedsheet ghosts in the classical sense. But their walls were heavy with the kind of poison that seeps from broken dreams.

Yes, there were bumps in the night back then. Muffled footsteps across the carpeted upper floors while everyone was downstairs. Odd, barely perceptible shapes altering the shafts of sunlight as it finally reached high enough into the sky to peep out from behind blocks of flats that loomed like concrete coffins stacked all in a row. Live burials intended to house the sorts of people that society would rather forget.

For me the indelible brand of my working class roots will forever dictate how I see the magickal world. Sorcery of any discipline is bound up with the spirit of place, and this is doubly true of those systems that directly interface with the history of a given area or its people. So yes, all my houses were most definitely haunted while I was growing up. It is just that some of those unfulfilled spirits were still very much alive.

Haunted Homes

It is interesting to see the uninitiated masses self diagnoses a haunting based on little real evidence. Odd noises late at night, cold spots and fleeting glimpses of some dark and shadowy figure out of the corner of the eye. Sleep paralysis and the old hag sitting on their chests. Shadow people. Black dogs. These then are what the average person expects to experience when dealing with the discarnate.

Videos go viral on any number of online streaming platforms, each showing the gradual escalation of the dead towards the dangerous while all too mundane likes and shares roll in. Pictures fall from walls and mirrors break. Both children and animals are put in harms way as cupboard doors drift open, drawers too, sending their contents spinning towards the sky.

Of course it is best for the viewer to ignore the obvious sound of compressed air being triggered as they do so. Or how the child seems to have been coached on the correct way to describe the little old lady with missing skin that lives in the basement. The fear being shown by pets in these supposedly active locations is easy enough to explain with silent dog whistles or masks worn off screen too.

Cruelty for clout it seems, as has ever been the way of things. There are as many reasons for fakery as there are people trying to convince their audiences that the ghosts are all too real. Yet this drift towards the home directly manifesting as horror fiction is not the fault of laypeople from outside of the necromantic sphere, not when the cultural narrative has always been one of fearing the unknown.

Despite the literary hype violent or at least physically active hauntings are actually quite rare. The dead, be they the spirits of those who have gone before or the ghostforms that represent their personality rendered down to a coldly calculating thoughtform as the brain dies, are always watching. But that does not mean that they are also waiting to create as much damage as possible while Satan himself laughs from the shadows.

Folklore and reality rarely intersect in such a way, at least according to those who find comfort in normality. They would state that the mundane provides the most realistic answer for such flamboyant manifestations, and more often then not they would be right. But the accelerated necromancer exists in the grey area created when all those explanations prove to be a poor panacea for the fear of the unknown.

Cold spots are just badly insulated windows. Creaking stairs are nothing more than the house settling. Bangs in the walls are incorrectly installed water pipes. And the pale white figure in a full wedding dress and bloody veil looming over the bed while the resident sleeps is simply a nightmare and nothing more. There are as many compelling arguments as to why this must be the case as there are phenomena to explain.

The necromancer recognises that not everything that howls in the night is a product of the cemetery, though that does not make it any less of a part of the rich tapestry of death current phenomenon. As a representation of the sum total of human and cultural experience with relation to the spirit world it must also include all of the false positives simply by virtue of their attribution to the unseen.

People have long been indoctrinated by both religion and popular culture to fear the supernatural of course. And while a little wariness may be wise when encountering ghostforms or echoes in the wild, the indelible fact remains that the terror fuelled reaction to most of those bizarre visitations is really caused by a lack of information.

In the West the now ascendant Protestant Christianity that took hold of the American psyche during the 20th Century has a lot to answer for here. Claims that all ghosts are demons in disguise to correct the faulty logic of that denomination's holy book coupled with the ease at which a few ultra-conservatives bought up vast tracts of modern media to spread propaganda directly contributes to this ongoing error.

All houses are haunted in their own way. Memories hang in the air, adding fleeting shadows to the vision of those who once experienced the events now half forgotten. History has a certain sound, explosions of silence, audible absence, the crushing weight of years. And the dead fit into this tapestry all too easily, because in many cases there were there first.

How few among the uninitiated could live with the concrete knowledge that they are never, ever alone. The embarrassment, fear of exposure. Hidden actions brought to light. The realisation that even the walls and doors of their home are but illusions to the ever mobile ghostform or echo. Holographic representations of a virtual world, and constant images of the longed for life now most definitely over.

Perhaps it is better to just accept that all locations have their unseen inhabitants, new and old. Whether lived in for decades or newly inhabited. The spirits are echoes and shards of lives once lived, and the inhabitants will bring those ghostly memories and astral parasites with them as they rent and buy building after building. The background blotting paper of reality loves picking up the stains of emotion after all.

That is rarely a problem though, despite what the mainstream media or hack horror novelists will say to the contrary. While some seemingly malevolent entities are best either avoided or removed from a given location, the invisible and more importantly incorporeal interlopers that generally make up the main body of such hauntings are absolutely harmless. Best not to kick the bear, then, and leave well alone.

The occasional fleeting shadow, muffled bump, oddly polite jump scare. These are the signs of their passing. Ghosts or ghostforms, stone tape recordings or shards. Even poltergeists or echoes. All this is just terminology, words the uninitiated and accelerated necromancer alike have put in place to try and name and tame the immaterial. And as with necrogeography, the map is never the territory.

Those titles are as meaningless in the grand narrative of things as the rights of ownership over a certain plot of land and the brickwork erected upon it. As the wind or rain are accepted to be natural by the average person so should the ever present background hum of the spirit world too, because those wisp like strands of loose information not going away anytime soon.

Clearing A Space

House clearing, in the more mundane sense, is the act of removing the contents of a home to either storage or the rubbish dump. Perhaps the occupant has died, or moved on into assisted living. Maybe they are overwhelmed by the memories the ever accumulating hoard of curios and trinkets represent and just need a fresh start. Regardless of the details there is value to be found in this change.

The location is stripped back to the raw, empty floors and the past is dragged out kicking and screaming into the skip with the tables, chairs and damp boxes of old newspapers. As an accelerated necromancer I understand this concept all too well, though in my case it is energies and not family heirlooms that I am occasionally forced to remove. Because live and let live rarely applies to the malicious dead.

While the integrity of the Veil is rarely questioned, acting as it does as a mostly inert storehouse of personality and information, the fact remains that some fail to make the trip. Of these unseen stragglers both ghostforms and echoes are the most potentially problematic, while shards are rarely an issue due to their status as little better than place memory replayed by untrained mediums or overwrought teens.

In general the wandering dead have free access to most spaces within the material realm, and only those with suitable wards or which experience regular cleansing and banishing will be mostly free of their presence. But this secondary layer to the background hum of a given location is rarely ever an issue unless the people living there have started to find themselves under some form of energetic or emotional assault.

Should the necromancer suspect an infestation of astral parasites the first and most important act is to diagnose their presence, as well as gaining a feel for what exactly they are. More psychically attuned adepts can do this pretty easily by just paying the family a visit and drinking in the atmosphere, though less skilled priests and priestesses of the veil have another, slightly slower option.

A small bowl of salt can be placed in an easily viewable corner away from sources of both moisture and potential contact with pets. Any changes are noted over the next week, and while tales of this crystal turning black in the presence of spirits are mostly false they will dull towards yellow if the space is active. While this does not give any real insight into the type of pseudo-entity that at the location it is enough to make a start.

Once diagnosed the actual work to remove them will begin. A suitably skilled adept may be able to parlay with the entities in the building, convincing them to seek an easier meal elsewhere or face the full might of their ritualistic know-how. This may seem to be a negative act, and few will admit to passing the problem to someone else in such a way, yet this is exactly how the banishing process really works.

There is no light to send them to, and no simple way to destroy them either. All that can be done is to keep those who ask for help safe while trying to minimise the damage that can be seen. And while there are ample sources available describing different cleansing blends, be they for home or human, the uncomfortable truth is that the pseudo-entities that remain on this side of the Veil are going to do so until they starve.

191

Perhaps the more stubborn of those who drift along the underworld ley lines which criss-cross the built environment will put up a fight when being asked to leave their current rest stop on that eternal journey. Scavenging animals will fight to protect their food source from being taken from them, true, but only so much. Once a larger predator makes itself known in the clearing the smaller creatures tend to scurry away.

As such the adept who has previously made pacts with the gods, goddesses or psychopomps of the underworld could call upon them to remove the unwanted pests. Any personal egregores or servitors which specialise in combat are also an option, though may need to actually make their presence known during the conversation to have the same bargaining power as name dropping the chthonic spirits of old.

Even in victory the accelerated necromancer has an eye on the next skirmish, and understands that the only way to keep such forces from returning is to focus on the very esoteric dust piles that have granted the invading entities a foothold in the first place. Because no matter how good the medium or wily the adept, a spiritually dirty space will always attract more visitors once the current crop have been expelled.

A full space clearing starts like any other spring clean. In fact, many of the tasks undertaken are of benefit on a purely mundane level, though when coupled with a strong will to be free of the issues which have been plaguing a given building they become ritualistic endeavours in their own right. Lest the adept ever forget that it is intent and not barbaric words or heirloom trinkets that make magick really work.

The idea behind this extremely pragmatic methodology is to simply and effectively disrupt the energetic background hum that may have attracted the ghostform, or more likely echo, in the first place. The latter seem to be especially tied to the physical state of the rooms that they drift through looking for a meal, and if this is sufficiently altered then they will likely lose interest and move on anyway.

Loose rugs should be taken outside if at all possible and aired in the sunlight, and it is likely a good opportunity to do the same with the curtains or blinds as well if possible. Throws, sofa covers and supposedly haunted objects are also best cleansed under those warming, golden rays, as the damp that can creep into fabrics overnight renders the usual full moon methodology problematic.

Once these are all safely out of the way the floors should be swept or vacuumed, shelves dusted and all windows opened to allow a strong breeze to blow through the stagnant air. Bells can be rung at this point, or music played just loud enough to further vibrate the atmosphere without pushing any neighbours to the brink of calling the police. Rhythmic beats are best here, with heavy baselines and thumping drums.

Frankincense can be burned in stick, cone or even resin form and will soon fill the entire space, while those of a kitchen witch persuasion can bake bread or scones and add that warming fire element to the rising perfume now dominating the home. If possible the entire living area should be rearranged, moving the sofas and cabinets around to further confound those entities that were far happier the way things were.

Indeed this is one of the main reasons why supernatural folklore is awash with tales of people encountering resistance from the unseen world while renovating old buildings, or redecorating after just moving in. It rarely has anything to do with the previous inhabitants and their preference for lilac wallpaper, despite what those ghostforms may say when questioned, and all to do with them realising that their time is now up.

The more a location changes, the harder it is for the astral parasites not quite living there to maintain their grip on the space. As the energy evolves into an expression of the new inhabitant's still mortal hopes, dreams and slowly accreting memories, the more the soup of past events or stagnant solitude that the echoes require to remain tethered there are overwritten.

Ultimately a strong understanding of what they actually are actively dis-empowers the entities involved. Because if the pseudo-spirits that usually crowd around such locations are but animalistic bundles of stray thoughts given some sort of very limited agency in the material plane then they should not be granted a level of terror based respect that they do not deserve.

Parties, games nights, friends over to watch films and laughter filling the air. The boisterousness of one too many beers and rock music until the early hours. Stolen kisses and midnight pizza. Dancing in the garden while the house behind them shakes with the vibrancy of life. This, then, is the best and most honest of all banishing techniques. Nothing removes a ghostform or echo as quickly as refusing to let them win.

Necrohexing

Honestly I feel no shame for taking action against those who cross me. Maybe it is a holdover from my naive interest in more traditional left hand path religions when I was first dabbling in sorcery all those years ago, but I have never been the best at turning the other cheek. It would be disingenuous not to admit that the necromantic arts lend themselves to such occasionally petty reprisals, after all.

Have a care, though. Cursing or otherwise attacking a target in this way should only be undertaken when there is a genuine need. Such self control is a necessity for the priest or priestess of the Veil who wishes to maintain the moral standing such a respectable title claims, as well as keeping themselves from falling into paranoia and toxicity at the slightest provocation too. Balance first, revenge when there is no other choice.

After an understanding of the unseen is gained the adept can start to put those forces to work in their practice. And while accelerated necromancy attempts to be a positive influence on the material world, holding the balance as sacred necessitates the creation of tools to both help and harm depending on how that universal pendulum is swinging at the time.

Hexing within this system falls into two main conceptual strands. The first utilises the energetic aspects of the death current in a manner not dissimilar to how the darker edge of the witchcraft tradition deals with trouble, while the second calls upon the denizens of the spiritual realm as mercenaries of sorts, thereby outsourcing the heavy lifting to others instead.

For solo efforts, the plague hex is a simple and effective way to even the score. Relying heavily on grave glass, itself a staple ingredient within most necromantic operations, it uses those bottle green chips as both a metaphysical focal point and small battery of stored cemetery essence. And in this they have no equal.

If the adept is looking to bring their enemies low with mystery ailments that have no known cause or cure then those sharp little fragments are the key. First, a small clay figure is created to represent the victim. As this operation relies upon old fashioned image magick it should also include something from their body, be it nail trimmings, eye lashes or lost hair. Blood would be best, though is obviously quite difficult to get.

If this is not possible then a tiny ball of paper with their real name written on it will do, though perhaps a photograph would be better. A shard of grave glass is then pressed into the human effigy in the position of each of their vital organs, forced through from back to front until the figurine takes on a suitably macabre and agonised appearance. A sample chant while applying the sharp fragments to the clay is outlined below.

"Fates, blade to skin.

Furies, edge to bone.

Nemesis, hook to marrow.

Pull the needle through."

As the glass leaches its payload of cooling cemetery essence into the surrounding clay, so will the health of the necromancer's target begin to wane, only improving should mercy win out over anger and a decision made to end the ritual early. This is as simple as breaking up the human shape, before returning the bottle green chips of entropic force to the soil. The rough clay can then be buried in the same hole too.

For those who fear that their good nature will allow the suffering of the target to influence the eventual duration of such a slow motion assassination, the methodology can be altered slightly to prevent such a change of heart. In these cases the plague hex is crafted almost the same way, but the effigy is placed in a black sackcloth pouch and dropped into a deep but open grave where it would be impossible to retrieve.

If creating such a clay effigy is too difficult a task, or the required ingredients are unavailable, then a much more scattergun approach may work. Again the name of the victim is added to a small peace of paper and this is rolled to form a seed. A drop of the necromancer's own blood is used to seal this bundle and it is sown into the earth beside a fresh burial where it will hopefully draw the attention of the cemetery.

The carrion hex relies upon the adept's ability to visualise the person who wronged them and overlay that image onto a hunk of fresh meat, usually pork or beef as these are relatively safe to handle raw. Their name is then cut or burned into the still oozing protein, before it is deposited in a quiet corner of the cemetery for scavengers, both living and dead, to feast upon.

As this is ripped to shreds, consumed and digested so too will the health of the victim begin to spiral into accelerated decay. This hex can also prove useful for those seeking domination as opposed to destruction. If the priest or priestess of the Veil only wishes to subjugate their enemies instead of fatally wounding them then the meat can be cooked as rare as is safe and eaten by the necromancer themselves.

Yes, the spirits of the graveyard can be recruited to do damage on behalf of the living too. Echoes, the barely animalistic potential poltergeists that are usually found feeding off the sorrow of those thinking about the dead can be put to work relatively easily through a procession hex, as long as the target lives nearby enough to make such a ritual viable.

Once a suitably active spot in the cemetery is found a grand invitation is extended to any who dwell within that are looking for a more comfortable home than marble and mud can provide. These are then bid to follow the adept, and taken on a nocturnal walk through the back alleys and winding streets to the living space of the eventual target. Some will, many will not, but at least a few should be interested.

Grave dirt is dropped along the route every so often as the necromancer walks to keep the likely slowly diminishing pack of astral leeches from returning to their former home within the graveyard too early, and a line of this is left beneath the front door once they arrive at the destination as a marker. Residency in the building is offered and the necromancer makes a hasty retreat in the hopes that some decide to stay.

Alternatively, should this be too far away to maintain the attention of those astral parasites as the procession hex winds its way towards the eventual destination a wraith jar can be mailed to the location instead. Care should be taken to remove all identifying marks and forensic evidence though, as this may constitute a crime in certain jurisdictions. As such it is better to construct these postal ones without the adept's blood or hair.

In more extreme cases the graveyard's inhabitants can be roused into direct action, should the location itself have suffered the heavy hand of vandals or the untrained toilet habits of the local drunk population. This kind of damage usually reigns unchecked due to the unravelling of the guardian who once watched over the sacred space, or the conversion of the entire plot of land to some form of municipal park instead.

Lost, angry and starving, the echoes in these blighted locations are little better than feral monsters, open to manipulation by a wily necromancer with a score to settle This, then, is the scavenger hex, and it works especially well if the people to be targeted are a local street gang, social group or individual that regularly moves through that location.

The methodology is genuinely simple. The adept need only make verbal contact with the few broken dryads who try to cling to life despite the stinking urine, burnt roots and torn strips of bark, convincing them that the person responsible for all the recent damage within the cemetery bounds needs to be punished for those crimes. And that the blame, of course, lies with the necromancer's intended victim.

Intimately wired into the surrounding landscape by virtue of their massive root network, these nature and death current hybrids will pass that information on to the others who dwell within the low stone walls, adding to the chance that the next walk through the headstones that the target takes is less than pleasant.

This is a rare necrohex that can be shifted in tone towards overtly positive ends. Efforts to rouse the inhabitants of a cemetery towards taking back their land from violent or disinterested interlopers who see the entire space as either a garbage dump or open sewer is never a bad thing.

Have a care, though, for while a space can be rendered sacred again through such an uprising, the work of the adept does not end there. A graveyard guardian is unlikely to reform for many years after the destructive elements of the uninitiated public have left. And if the necromancer seeks to keep that waypoint running in a more harmonious fashion then they will need to take that role onboard for themselves while alive.

Thrills And Chills

Ghost hunts can be surprisingly boring affairs, especially if any of the entities said to roam those usually cavernous and draughty locations are dormant when you arrive. And unfortunately moving alone in the shadows and deliberately stepping out when the rest of the party are nearby is only funny the first dozen or so times. Less said about the way I was forced to wear a glow stick after that the better.

Of course I know of a few other ways to make a visit more interesting. Necromancers come preprepared with a suite of abilities that can push a location further towards the weird if we so choose. And considering that the rest of the participants are supposedly there to witness something spooky it would be rude not to give that spiritual revelation the very best chance of occurring.

And for those of you who have no interest in paranormal investigation as a hobby the following tricks can be utilised in a ritualistic setting just as easily, though I would recommend that any doorways opened are subsequently closed as soon as your work is done. Especially true if the location is either your home, or someone else's. Balance above all things, after all.

In Defence Of Ouija

Of all the tools that the general public have adopted to do the adept's job for them, the Ouija board is by far the most controversial. A ritual in a box and uniquely sold within the games section of almost every large toy store, this alphabetic portal to the unseen world is a staple of modern horror fiction. Yet the real dangers of using the board stem not from the planchette but the humans holding it instead.

Seen by outsiders as needlessly dangerous, a series of frankly arbitrary rules designed to mitigate those unfounded fears would become cultural cannon during the Satanic panic of the 1980's. While some of these, such as showing the spirits all due respect when calling upon them or avoiding the thing entirely if under the influence of drugs and alcohol actually make sense, others are just ridiculous religious fantasies.

The truth is that yes, demons can be summoned with the board, but both hidden intent and lack of definition are key factors which contribute to such an illuminating misstep. As with much within the esoteric space the Ouija can serve as a viable link to the infernal just as easily as the ghostly, yet has no polarity of its own. It is the fear of evil that allows such negative forces to hijack the call, a very human problem indeed.

Hidden biases can be deadly, which is why the adept is encouraged to face down such personality quirks before embarking on any serious ritual. They are also advised to come to terms with their own ghostform through shadow work, a sometimes difficult task. But the average user of the board, be they weekend parapsychologists or full time hobbyists, are unlikely to have such a steely control over those instincts.

So in the end a subconscious fear that all spirits are really demons is the issue, not the board itself. Prior programming, both religious and cultural, has led to a situation where the uninitiated majority who dabble in such things dwell in an oddly liminal state, feeling short changed if something infernal does not appear to haunt their home after the candles are blown out, and terrified of being killed if it actually does.

Conversely, successful use of the Ouija board is shown to rely upon the focussed input of those wielding it and a mastery of their unconscious biases towards certain anticipated, or perhaps feared, results. While this attitude is key to self preservation when dealing with such potentially unruly forces in general, it also produces the most authentic conversations too.

So no, the cardboard and plastic are not seeded with demonic essence at the factory in China where they are churned out by the thousand. There is no conspiracy to destroy the faith of the American youth, nor are European teens any more likely to acquire a demonic ride along using the Ouija than they are attending their local seminary. It is religious programming which instead causes those issues through dogma and censure.

No matter how hard the scaremongering fundamentalists would push that narrative to protect the next generation from having a mere second of fun, the actual reason as to why so many troubled teens encounter something horrific while playing with the planchette in their dorm rooms after hours is due to the inherently pious worldview that unknowingly attaches itself the requests being sent out. It is just that simple.

Worse, by colouring those once personal cross-Veil interactions with a heavy smear of transgression it actively attracts those who would wish to deliberately seek the demonic between the letters. There is nothing wrong with approaching the infernal powers in a purely ritualistic setting of course. They are not necessarily evil, just mired in their own agendas. But bothering them as a rite of passage is risky at best.

Biblical thought is on the rise in paranormal investigation. This is due to both the caustic influence of Spiritualism, itself a Christian heresy, and the American domination of the televised ghost hunting space. The conservative underpinning of much of the education in that nation, coupled with personal opinion on haunted matters by a few famous charlatans now taken as fact, is warping the entire field globally.

And even if the adept has little interest in organised ghost hunting they will no doubt have felt the damage dealt to the more spiritual aspects of haunted homes by these self appointed watchdogs. Senators and lay preachers dripping in smug snake oil, engaged in spiritual warfare over lands which were never theirs to carve up in the first place. Policing the human need to engage with the Otherworld like the inquisition of old.

While hardcore sceptics and the associated scientific community can be completely disregarded by virtue of their almost global vetoing of anything even approaching the supernatural, those claiming the title of agnostic are really now anything but. The religious dial has moved so far towards fundamentalism in recent decades that even those who consider themselves to be unsure are now just mired in its wake by default.

The wholesale demonising of Ouija by the more blinkered Christian voices and the widespread adoption of those fundamentalist biases by the wider public is a perfect illustration of the ability of conservative owned media to manipulate the masses, even those of differing faiths or none at all. This is an issue that extends far beyond mere necromancy, and bleeds into the darker edges of the esoteric cultural space as well.

Some who consider themselves witches have unknowingly absorbed those draconian views of the spirit world, and would prefer to call on lofty saints than earth bound ancestors anyway. Those too may face the demonic when making a collect call to somewhere not quite nearby on the board, and a good indicator of whether this will be the case can be seen as soon as they sit at the table.

A prayer to Saint Michael or similar celestial proxies when opening the Ouija is a dead giveaway that the witch, medium or hobbyist has become a carrier for the ghosts as demons bias and is attempting to mitigate the very problem that they are themselves unknowingly going to cause. The adept should be especially careful around such people, and seek to distance themselves from the ensuing chaos ahead of time.

A proper tone from the point of view of accelerated necromancy would be one of reverence for the psychopomps of old and the goddesses who preside over the underworlds that are being called upon to chat. It would remind the living in attendance that the dead who will soon be arriving are doing so under oath to behave respectfully in exchange for reverence from those holding the planchette during the call.

The adept should drive home the point to all assembled that the infernal are busy with their own matters and just do not have either the time or inclination to hover around a slab of cardboard and plastic awaiting the chance to ruin people's lives. These awesome and far from evil once were gods only come when called, so as long as the hidden biases of the living do not cause a misdial then there is little to really fear.

Ultimately, none who walk the cemetery path should fall into the potentially fatal error that all ghosts must be demons in disguise because an old book that in truth has nothing to do with their choice to explore things unseen said so. Such self fulfilling prophecies may make for great television, adding to the background hum of misinformation about what exactly the Ouija board really makes contact with, but are otherwise useless.

Accelerated Seances

Not everyone who works with spirits on an esoteric level will be inter-
ested in paranormal investigation during the downtime from their mundane
lives. Maybe a more mediumistic paradigm is preferred. Or perhaps the
reason for interest in the necromantic path is specifically to help mitigate
the issues which the dead are causing in their life right here, right now.

There is nothing wrong with that narrow focus. I too feel that way some-
times. Years of research would eventually lead me to stop viewing the ma-
jority of things which go bump in the night as deceased loved ones, framing
them as errant strands of information seeking to persist within a hostile
environment instead. But even I still venture forth to sit in the company of
strangers occasionally for old times sake.

The accelerated necromancer is uniquely poised to assist their community in matters unseen. A solemn but fruitful calling, it is their role in life to
keep the living and the dead apart by striking an acceptable balance between
the needs of those otherwise fundamentally opposed camps. Yet there are
times when the uninitiated majority are of use in return, especially if the Veil
is to be pierced for answers.

Such operations require a lot of energy, both mental and bioelectric. No
matter how skilled a medium this level of effort may be too much for single adepts to maintain on their own for any length of time. Because make
no mistake to force contact with those happily dwelling on the other side,
regardless of what form that resting place is thought to take, requires dedicated group effort focussed through a priestly lens.

In general terms there are two differing views of the afterlife when discussing the actual non-physical location that houses the personality after
death. This dual distinction is purely for those who successfully moved beyond the mundane realm of course, and does not take into account the many
wandering entities trapped within the physical plane. They are a local issue,
and one that is better addressed separately.

The classical version adopted by most esoteric traditions states that those
who have crossed over inhabit some form of alternate realm, pottering

around next to mist choked rivers under permanently sunny skies while the living continue on at something approaching the same speed without them. Think Roman Avernus, Greek Elysium or Norse Hel. Spirits held here retain some agency and would be relatively easy to contact.

The variation adopted by accelerated necromancers considers the dead to be a sum total of the information which once made up the mind as it returns to an inert state stored within the womb of Tiamat. This version of the Otherworld has more in common with a computer hard drive, and those not quite digital souls have no semblance of continued life over there without the input of a living creature who decides to access them.

Time for these imprints is also stationary unless they are being channelled by an adept in the current era, and it can be assumed that any knowledge on worldly matters is very much a reflection of their original lived experience only. Those who exist outside of unfolding events cannot offer comment on the vagaries which develop during the ever quickening forward march of modernity, after all.

Regardless of the necromancer's chosen flavour the methods for actually interfacing with either variation of the Otherworld through group ritual remain largely the same. Any esoteric distinctions are more a matter of language than reality, and one which causes surprisingly little difference in how those entities are handled during the exploration of the chthonic realms themselves.

The evening begins with the necromancer and a group of associates sitting around a table. There is no need to hold hands or touch fingers as with the Spiritualists of old, because a length of copper chain is instead used to raise the power within the circle, removing the need for physical contact among strangers. This was always a contentious part of classic séances, causing lapses of concentration at very inconvenient times.

A natural conductor, copper has a long history of use in esoteric traditions as a method of raising and circulating energy. Ritual knives have been crafted from this metal for centuries, and on a more mundane level it regularly finds use in jewellery designed to help with a variety of inflammatory conditions such as arthritis. Antibacterial, this red-brown element can also be easily cleaned between uses.

While silver appears to be a better option for the chain at first, this may in fact repel any forces that are gathering around the table due to its stridently protective properties. While there is a benefit to keeping the less desirable entities in a location away from the sitters, such a blanket ban will only hinder the broad range of potential results.

Séances within the necromantic framework adopted by the accelerated adept are not generally considered to be an efficient way to make contact with the ghostforms, echoes and shards that are drifting loose within the actual location itself. Natural psychic abilities are a better tool for such localised discourse, as talking to the resident dead rarely requires the added energetic element created during group workings.

No, these sittings are deliberately targeted affairs, conducted to foster discourse with a named ancestor or ask a series of very specific questions which have need of answers instead. Group work in a public setting can be a little less results focussed, though ritualistic endeavours among adepts should have an underlying goal in mind. Just proving the existence of the Otherworld is not enough to warrant all that effort.

The copper chain is held in the gently closed fists of all those in the circle against the table, while the spare ends are loosely wrapped around the necromancer's wrists with enough redundancy to allow for some movement by everyone taking part. Thus the actual body and nervous system of the person who will be actively piercing the Veil makes up the closing clasp of the ritual circle.

Opening rites are conducted in two stages, firstly with the adept alone before the rest of the group are seated and then once everyone is comfortable. These can be tailored to the specific goddesses or helper spirits which are preferred, and while there are a number of different options the following calling is a good catch all example that should at least hint at the general tone being sought by both chants.

"Psychopomps and torch-bearers, heed my steps.

One in front of the other, descend and explore.

My heartbeat a drum that resists your embrace.

My name is ___ should we meet again.

Psychopomps and torch-bearers, light my way.

Gates are opened and my mind journeys on.

Let me see the beauty of your chthonic mansions.

My name is ___ should we meet again.

Psychopomps and torch-bearers, grant me celerity.

To hold audience with your charges dwelling below.

But guide me home once I have heard their stories.

My name is ___ should we meet again."

This is recited as many times as is necessary to allow the necromancer to enter the required hypnogogic state of mind. A metronome can be situated within their eyeline to aid in the pacing of the words, as well as for its own calming effect. And the sitters can be encouraged to join in as well, quietly copying the calling but substituting their own name at the end if they feel comfortable enough to do so.

All the while the energy in the room continues to rise even as the adept themselves fall inwards, offering their vocal chords up as a mouthpeace for the voices of those who have gone before. Here too the séance becomes a team effort, as with the priest or priestess of the Veil being the one who has chosen to journey below in such a way someone else needs to actually ask questions of the dead speaking through them.

Thus as with the duels of bygone days there must be a second, someone to both make sure that the discussion is held in a safe and productive manner and also that the necromancer is able to return to the material realm. This need not be an active participant in the ritual itself, and indeed there is some evidence that standing apart from the circle helps to foster objectivity when taking part in such disjointed discourse.

Should the adept lose themselves to the trance like state and fail to begin the journey back upwards from the vaulted caverns of the Otherworld then this master of ceremonies also has the power to end the séance at any time through a simple unbinding of the chains wrapped around the necromancer's wrists. This can be tricky if the priest or priestess of the Veil is particularly animated when possessed, so care should be taken.

It does not cause an instant end to the proceedings of course, though once the adept's bioelectric battery is exhausted they will sluggishly regain their senses. Tales of mediums being permanently possessed or dragged screaming into the abyss below are thankfully just folklore. There is little risk to the traveller when their physical shell is still intact, and those chthonic mansions dislike overnight visitors anyway.

Indeed once the séance is ready to bring to a close the second will begin to question the adept on what they can see, and where they are. A staircase lined with the torches of the psychopomps called upon in the earlier chants should be looked for, and those spirits may also be in attendance. If they choose to help usher the traveller back towards the material realm then all the better, though it is never guaranteed.

This climb back to reality can take a while, and the priest or priestess of the Veil will likely be both groggy and drained when finally returning to waking consciousness. It is not recommended that they drive or use heavy machinery for at least a full day afterwards, because as with all necromantic rituals the traveller will bring a little piece of the Otherworld back with them.

The séance can then be ended and those in attendance allowed to disperse. As with the ritualistic endeavours of the early chaos magickians the best way to banish is with laughter, and nothing else quite eases the minds of slightly spooked outsiders than a little gallows humour. It also covers up the fact that there is no elaborate closing of the sacred space like many in the room may expect, as that is what the chain is for.

Not only does this help maintain a constant flow of energy should someone decide to break the circle and make an early exit during the ritual, but is also allows for the adept to return the area to mundane reality by simply rolling the metallic links back into a ball and taking them home. A few days immersed in tomb wash will clear the chthonic signature of the operation from the copper and render it as good as new.

On rare occasions where this does not feel enough to fully disperse the energy which was raised during the night's esoteric entertainment, then a quick and dirty banishing will usually suffice to forcefully remove the lingering essence of the Otherworld from the room in which it was held. This is best done before the adept leaves the building at the end of the night so as to not leave a potential problem for others behind.

A note on the choice of second, however. While the necromancer has little to fear from either possession or damnation while traversing the Otherworld, a trustworthy associate is a must for any operation which leaves the adept's flesh and blood body vulnerable to assault while their mind is elsewhere. As such someone who will quickly jump to their defence should the living act on the antagonising words of the dead is preferred.

Yes, the accelerated séance is literally just ritual invocation without the need for a skilled group of sorcerers to carry the extra weight. Such a hot-wiring of what is usually a far more involved process could definitely be considered unsafe, though it is assumed that the adept will have previous experience travelling those internal roads to the Otherworld before their first night as presiding medium is held.

In truth the biggest sleight of hand comes into play when convincing the uninitiated sitting at the table that their bioelectric energy is being spent on nothing more than an interesting parlour trick, when in fact they are being drained to aid the accelerated necromancer and their second in finding out specific information. Not that it really matters, of course, as it is doubtful that they could recognise the difference either way.

Claiming A Graveyard

Ah yes, I have claimed many a graveyard in my time. Whole cemeteries, hundreds of burials. All the better to stand among the shadows and make peace with the energies that coalesce there before putting them to work. Of course, such holds upon those blighted plots of land are only ever fleeting, and also most definitely non-exclusive too. Because who knows how many necromancers, witches and sorcerers also did the same.

I successfully gained my personal passport to the yawning gateways of the underworld, and in the end that is all that really matters. But that boon came with a guardianship of those inside the low stone walls, custody of the bodies who had found their final resting places there, and a healthy dose of disdain for the living who would walk those gravel trackways without the required respect.

Not every accelerated adept can commit to the hours of exploration that are required to give an honest and balanced overview of the thin places which cluster around their urban home. Necrogeography is nothing more than just one tool among many that the priest or priestess of the Veil can use to better grow their connection to the death current. And should time be an issue then perhaps it is better to try something else.

Even the more mobile necromancer may be looking for a permanent base among the gravestones as well, a waypoint of their very own which allows for a more personal relationship with the spirits of the corpse ways. While friendships with those chaotic echoes is highly unlikely, a grudging respect can still be attained if the traveller is willing to give the dead their due over repeated visits.

After a few trips around the local area, either necrogeographic or mundane, the most energetically active graveyard is chosen to become the staging ground for future endeavours. Far from just serving as a ritualistic launch pad, the ground will become a place of respite and healing as the adept falls back on their ghoulish hunger to get through the day.

The first and most important action that the necromancer completes when entering their chosen cemetery while looking to initially stake a claim is one of respectful petition. An offering to those who already hold ownership over the space, be they living or dead, is completed. And just like with the fare for the ferryman it falls to coins to pay that tithe.

The adept begins the ritual by standing somewhere as close to the entrance as possible, but still outside of the range of prying eyes. Copper coins are then produced from their knapsack, a number representative of all their previous visits and past due payment for that earlier hospitality. These are then flicked into the nearest hedge or overgrown line of bushes, while an opening similar to the following example is intoned.

"My name is ___ and I am no threat to you.

I come to tarry awhile in the oak tree shade.

Do not bar my passage because I still draw breath.

Or obscure these trackways while my heart beats.

Face me now if you would slow my passage.

Or bless my onward journey with your silence.

This is my right within these storied walls.

My name is ___ and I vow to do you no harm."

These actions are intent specific, as if the adept were expected to do this every time they entered a cemetery it could cause serious issues when their mortal companions are unaware of the chthonic aspect of the necromancer's life. As such, while all who respect the balance should tread lightly while drifting among the gravestones there is no need to petition the dead beneath unless a claim is being made.

Here the priest or priestess of the Veil may encounter resistance from the guardian of the graveyard, a egregore cast from the numerous fragments of memory still lying in the air around the headstones. Dog like, humanoid or even shaped like a bear, this pseudo-entity is tethered like Cerberus to the inner boundaries of the burial site. Visible as fleeting shadow or undetectable by the inner vision, it will definitely be there.

A truly difficult foe to overcome, their mere presence can drain the bio-electric field of an adept dry in mere minutes. If they are not willing to be reasoned with then the only option is to face those roiling spirals of echo and shard scraps down, and any necromancer who can keep walking forward while under such an assault will eventually find that the pressure subsides. That guardian will be far from gone, however.

Once the adept has either avoided or otherwise weathered the psychic attack at the entrance they move inside the graveyard and head towards the centre. Here they can rest for a while if needed, and survey the lay of the land. This can be easily ascertained via a paper map or digital device. Once ready a compass is used to find the four directions, north, south east and west as they fall within the boundaries of the site.

These are further broken down into the ordinal points that intersect them, and if done correctly eight lines not dissimilar in shape to a chaos star should be seen. The necromancer is especially interested in these secondary points during the claiming ritual as they form the corners, though it is also worth keeping a note of where those cardinal directions sit as well just in case that information becomes useful at a later date.

Starting out towards the northwest, the adept walks to the location that the imagined geographic line crosses the boundary wall of the cemetery, negotiating overgrown brambles, grave markers and pitfalls as they go. Here then they find a secluded and perhaps hedge shrouded place to sit, before piercing the index finger of their non-dominant hand with a sterile pin or medical lancet and dripping a few drops of blood to the soil.

A ritual chant is raised to the spirits of place here, albeit quietly, and while one can be created to suit the individual adept's own needs the following would form a good base to work from. Have a care, though, as the guardian may return at any time during this recital and begin to drain the necromancer of their vitality again if it does not like the tone of the words being spoken.

"My name is ___ and I call you to my side.

I lay this offering in the oak tree shade.

Witness how the pregnant soil takes my breath.

And the trackways drink the dew from my heart.

Face me now and guide my passage.

To bless my onward journey with your words.

This is my claim within these storied walls.

My name is ___ and I vow to keep you from harm."

As their breath is mentioned the adept bends down and exhales upon the ground in front of them, and once the chant is finished they stand up again, and continue back to the centre of the cemetery. They do not bandage their finger, as any extra blood that drips into the soil was predestined to be added to the overall working even before the first cut was made.

The necromancer then moves from the centre to the northeast corner and repeats the chant, reopening the needle punch on their index finger should they need to. Then they return to the middle of the graveyard again, and do the same for the southeast and southwest boundary points as marked on their map. This can take hours to complete, and it can be assumed that they will be both sore and tired by the end.

After all is done they walk with great and haughty air of assumed privilege to the same gate which they arrived through, and only when outside the walls do they show a mere second of weakness by binding the wound on their hand. This is because the dead, be they lonely ghosts or rogue information, respond best to shows of strength. This becomes a necessary guise when dealing with such base and bestial intelligences.

A week or so later, when the scab has healed enough that it no longer bleeds, the adept returns to the cemetery and enters through the same gate. This is done without any rhyme or ritual, nor are any respects paid in either coin or words. If they make it to the centre of the location unchallenged then they can assume that it worked and they are now an accepted master of that blighted soil.

It is possible that they still meet considerable resistance from the guardian or other spirits in the area, and if this happens they have two choices. Force the issue by rerunning the original ritual again hoping for a different outcome, or travel on to seek a more welcoming place elsewhere. And there is no shame in avoiding a fight should the outcome be little better than occupied land and an insurgent population.

Claimed graveyards are the perfect place to harvest ingredients, seek shelter or top up the auric batteries should the need arise. But no matter how skilled the necromancer becomes in their chosen disciplines they must always remember that they are more elected official than overall ruler. As such they should reciprocate those unlikely boons through mundane acts such as picking up litter or clearing fallen debris.

Staying Under The Radar

Transgressor. Abomination. Iconoclast. Yes, I am all of these in the eyes of the mainstream by virtue of my necromantic interests. The social mores of our still ostensibly conservative culture aside, the general mood among the bland majority, holding as they do to a purely mundane view of the universe, is one that has little time for the spiritual outside of whichever mainstream religion rules the local roost.

But I march ever onward, refusing to be forced to comply with a human monoculture that I hold in contempt. My decision to be open about what some will perceive as crimes against decency aside, not everyone who I met during those journeys into the esoteric underclass were as willing to put their neck in the noose as me. And perhaps, upon deeper reflection, such reticence to step out from the shadows is the right stance to take.

The priests and priestesses of the Veil who reverently walk along the cemetery path are unlikely to favour national laws over personal expression. With the secrets of life, death and perhaps some weirdly egregoric immortality all on the table they see no reason to let the opinions of others slow their quest for knowledge.

And while some choose to seek fame and recognition for their talents by working as mediums or psychics, talking heads on television documentaries or hosts for guided rituals at occult conventions, others prefer to remain hidden within cemetery bounds. For every adept that sees print, hundreds more toil at their altars in secret, forced into silence by the pressures of the modern world.

Perhaps this reticence to be seen harkens back to the more transgressive aspects of chaos magick, a strikingly different countercultural phenomenon that adds a sweet note of disharmony to this otherwise classical necromantic paradigm as it accelerates those dry bones towards the future. Or maybe the very idea of seeking enlightenment among the gravestones naturally attracts outsiders of various kinds.

While each adept is the arbiter of their own moral compass a sidelong glance towards the ever tilting balance will remain the most important consideration for those enlightened few that seek to stay in the Reaper's good graces. But the seven necromantic laws are just guidelines and nothing more. Safety naturally overrules piety when required, though such a decision is never made without good reason.

It is almost guaranteed that such a marrow black and bone white code of ethics will rarely align with the otherwise conservative viewpoint held by the wider society at large. Yet the deeply instinctual and unashamedly primal nature of the modern esoteric movement may well be what initially attracted those freethinkers to the churchyard in the first place.

The occult remains a difficult pill for the majority to swallow. While hauntings are finding an increasingly entrenched, if both alarmist and Christianised, foothold within the mainstream media witchcraft in general is still seen by many as something to be feared. A discipline which relies upon the bounty of Gaia as much as the psychology of mourning, accelerated necromancy is more Neopagan than most involved would admit.

Long have the torches and pitchforks been raised against the outsider within. And while the police may struggle to find a good enough reason to imprison the cautious adept for their nocturnal interests the court of public opinion needs not hold itself to the same exacting standards of evidence. The rabble are always on the lookout for a reason to be roused to action, and those who act differently make the perfect scapegoats.

Few priests and priestesses of the Veil can claim to be self made millionaires, and as a result of the reliance upon mundane work as well as close habitation with those who hold more mainstream religious or social views necessitates a lightness of touch when approaching the burial sites and thin places of the city. As with membership of any fringe organisation or underground movement secrecy is safety, after all.

While calling all who revel in Neopaganism and its aligned magickal movements out of the broom closet to be counted en masse would be interesting from a sociological point of view, it is highly unlikely that the world will ever be a safe enough place to do so. Lives are all too easily ruined as accusations swirl around social media, hushed workplace conversations and even street level gossip.

Worse, the very knapsack that allows the adept to stroll confidently into the shadows without fear of supernatural reprisal could also be seen as incriminating evidence when the steely eye of the law falls upon their practice. Bones, nails, dusts and powders. Knives and wands. Sources of flame and strangely swirling liquids. All of these are easily considered proof of either sacrilegious motives or potentially violent intent.

The Satanic panic is far from over, and law enforcement will still try their best to get what would likely be perceived as yet another crazy off the streets should the need arise. And that term is not used flippantly. Many who walk the numerous modern esoteric paths have underlying issues, quirks of thought or emotional scars. These can be scaffolded by the sorcery that they perform, but never fully healed.

Institutions that profit from attacking the outsider in their midst would likely give little credence to the necromancer's claims about conducting research with all due respect for the dead, that actual remains are not required for ritual and no graves were disturbed as the adept passed by. Should there also be any history of cognitive conditions that require medication to mitigate, then the accused is on very shaky ground.

Regardless of mental stability, talk of currents and ghostforms will fall on death ears, the reputation of the many faced Reaper brought low by the actions of people who should have been smart enough not to get caught in the first place. What the priest and priestess of the Veil does they do in secret, and they are not compelled to act outside of the shadows unless maintaining the balance becomes a pressing issue.

The public are perhaps warranted in their collective outrage at stumbling upon an adept with their muddy hands in the roots of their long planted family tree, though. A desecration the accelerated adept would also disavow, albeit without giving away their position as they did so. Better to silently shake the head in disgust that shout about those feelings among the uninitiated. No point being dragged to the same pyre.

This is doubly true if the necromancer is stupid enough to dress like a black metal band while harvesting supplies. With more socially acceptable forms of witchcraft holding their own against the overtly religious as they struggle for legitimacy, those people of the craft are unlikely to want to spring to the defence of aligned disciplines who bring the esoteric into disrepute through a lack of care.

This form of censure has happened before. Prominent esoteric voices silenced and mistreated during extended jail time, imprisoned for a laundry list of minor crimes when the major ones were too difficult to prove. Witch hunts in the media and an establishment all too happy to watch those who refused to comply with their overarching narrative face punishment for sins against the collective.

It is for the best that the accelerated adept be as nondescript and private in their practice as the situations which they find themselves in will allow. Yes, séances and ghost hunts can be a fun diversion. Claims of mainstream mediumistic abilities can create a palatable cover for the adept's more esoteric, and less acceptable, interests. Perhaps line their pockets somewhat too, though never at the cost of their safety.

But the risk remains as strong as ever despite the socially acceptable labels, necessitating some defensive planning ahead of time. A paper trail of sorts can be helpful should their homes be raided for evidence, especially with regards to human bones. These can be purchased legally in most Western countries, and proof of that fact in invaluable to prevent potential criminal proceedings in the future.

Cover stories and smart but inconspicuous clothing are a must when around the uninitiated, especially on paranormal investigations or when harvesting ingredients from cemetery grounds. But hidden pockets and unseen spaces within backpacks are not usually necessary when out and about. There is no need to fall into that level of paranoia when most people do not ever see beyond the ends of their own noses anyway.

The carrying of grave dirt and coffin nails once the trip is over can be done with cloth bags and linen pouches. Taking the odd animal bone here and there is unlikely to rouse suspicion. Removing some weeds and collecting litter around the cemetery may even raise a smile. Careful interaction with a given space will lead to repeated visits, though the necromancer should try to keep the dangers of detection in mind.

Duality of nature is the default state for those who hold the esoteric in high esteem. These voyagers at the fringes of acceptability are as likely to work in the civil service as they are supermarkets. Banking complaints or call centre sales. Self employed, out of work, all professions now have downtime hardwired into their shift structure. How the chthonic few choose to spend those days can create miracles.

But regardless of how much the adept ultimately has to lose by not keeping this inherent weirdness a secret the golden rule is as simple as it is vital to continued survival within a hostile culture. While they can allow those more mainstream mediumistic and perhaps even Neopagan interests to become widely known, the uninitiated should never be allowed to witness their truly necromantic side unless there is no other choice.

Apendicies

The Soul Of London

Those who find solace within the nocturnal veins of their home city tend to stop fearing what it has in store for them. A lack of reverence for the spirit of place can lead to some potentially dangerous situations, and it goes without saying that the drunks or junkies are but violent fleas living between the bone towers and cartilage fences of the ever present genius loci itself.

Some secrets should remain locked away beneath well worn pavements, because there are times when the need to know can drive an already shattered mind to attempt magick as dangerous as it is illuminating. This, then, is a parting gift to my readers, a journey along the rotting veins of the city as I recount the tale of my most mind bending necrogeographic exploit in old London town.

You see I was plagued by cryptic nightmares throughout my teens. As a result sleep was neither comforting or even particularly energising for me. So with little else to do I would walk the streets of my city, caffeine in hand, until too tired to carry on. And as the sun rose over the smog choked trees, I knew it was time to return home and try to get some fitful sleep in between the art projects that occupied my waking mind.

During the 1990's the East End of London was practically a partly demolished rookery, with nothing to really see except rusting docks and derelict lots that would one day become massively overpriced investment *properties under the blighted banner of urban regeneration. So I, like many before me, gravitated towards the glitz and glamour of West End via the Square Mile.*

Whether it was the lights that drew me in, or the persistent sounds of my fellow lost souls drifting between the night calmed office blocks and ever onwards towards Oxford Street, I soon made a game of darting between alleyways and through courtyards others would overlook.

Mapping and remapping the nervous system of that slumbering giant, avoiding crowded thoroughfares while attempting to gain entry to abandoned buildings that stood like hollow tumours in an otherwise utilitarian sprawl. And as an interest in magick grew to replace the thrill of just being in those derelict places I would strive to speak with the spirits of the land who congregated there instead.

The gremlins of rust who gnawed at the fabric of the city. Smog sylphs that danced like motes in the air, their ever watchful eyes blinking against the shafts of sunlight that criss-crossed the gloom. Gutter goblins that revelled in the trash piled high against the drains. And as the corpse ways beckoned I wondered the burial plots of London and loped through the broken dryad shaded gravestones for solace to.

Kensel Green, Highgate, even the sadly contested Crossbones and the Goose that called it home. Prime territory for all the echoes and shards a young mind could take. Ghostforms pushing everything normal through to the edges of meaning by their very presence along the cemetery path. In time this unconscious motion led me to move beyond the nervous system of London and into its dreams.

This playful connection to the city remained a constant well into my late 20's, though with life pulling me away to other places and the stresses of both failing relationships and mundane work cutting my free time to a minimum it eventually became little better than a dull memory of sanctuary and warmth.

London loved me. It was my home and no matter the upheaval I would always have a place to return to. As a Cockney I think I actually believed that, regardless of how stupid it now sounds to much older ears. Indoctrination perhaps, weakness of mind masquerading as strength of character, all wrapped up in a mythologised tribalism.

And then I fell in love with a woman who was only in London for a year.

Our relationship blossomed and she wanted me to move across the country with her once she was done. This coincided with some very heavy duty magicks, an ill advised ongoing ritual and numerous old emotional scars returning to the surface.

The timing was terrible, and despite my earlier trust in the permanence of the city I also knew that to leave was to do so with all bridges burned. There was going to be no way back to my old life if I chose to give it up under those circumstances. I faced the kind of decision that was bigger than myself, and highly time sensitive, demanding an answer from me despite being in no fit state to think.

And so I did something decidedly out of character. It is not in my nature to defer to a higher power, yet here was a perfect opportunity to ask the soul of London what I should do. Yes I was out of practice. The caffeine fuelled insomnia of my younger years had given way to almost restful sleep. My magickal life had turned towards necromancy and the dark goddess Lilith. I was too worn out to wander for hours under neon skies.

Yet I had come close to approaching the very genius loci of the city once before, and already knew how I would go about achieving something that most would not dare attempt. I recognised where corpse ways were. I had already seen the waypoints up close and personal. The only thing holding me back was fear itself.

All those years ago I had decided against continuing as the idea of opening my psyche up to such a super massive flow of information seemed too inherently dangerous to be worth trying. This time I had nothing to lose. I had to see if my city could offer any advice to one of its most dedicated of children in their time of need.

The reasons for me to leave were mounting daily, yet perhaps the connection to my home town would prove too strong to walk away. If that blighted hyperobject told me to stay I would, yet in the end that is not the way it turned out.

The ritual was simple. Looking to be in the same receptive, liminal state as before I deliberately had as little sleep as possible in the week leading up to my journey. Lacking the energy to walk the route I had in mind a fitting alternative was found, albeit one that was far more densely packed than the night time alleys of yesteryear.

The early morning Tube is a difficult vehicle to ride on a short commute, and staying on it for hours while exhausted creates an almost hypnotic drone that seeps into every corner of your mind. So back into the veins of the city I dove, like a virus hitching a ride on the very blood cells that circulated under its concrete skin.

I travelled to the far fringes of the London Underground, each target station overlaid on my guiding compass rose, the eight pointed star of chaos. A simple mantra describing my desire to speak with the soul of the city on my lips as I struggled to stay awake, mumbling like a drunkard as the hours ticked by.

No one could have known what I had in mind. Even if my slumped figure flashed across the screens in the central control room repeatedly throughout the day there was a precedent. Some choose to travel to all of the edges of the network for no other reason than to say they have seen it for themselves. Yet my reasoning was anything but so mundane.

Starting with the Northern Line I rode the rails as far up into that as I could, then the District line in the North East. Docklands Light Railway in the East, then again to the South East as the line has two spurs out by Dock-lands. After each train reached its final stop I would sit on the platform for a while, before re-boarding the carriage and heading back towards the centre to take the next train on my list.

The Victoria Line served me well towards the South, Piccadilly to the South West, District to the West and finally the Metropolitan to the North West. I then returned to the very top of the Northern Line where it all started and bisected the city like a scalpel via that to finish up at Embankment by early evening.

It was Cleopatra's needle I sought, long a tourist attraction and even longer a monument to human civilisation. Originally a twin of the one on display in New York's Central Park, unlike its cross-Atlantic counterpart the monolith in London was buried in sand for many years before it found its current home, and this cool chthonic energy is palpable even on summer days. This, then, is the queen of London waypoints.

Sitting perched as it was on the banks of the Thames at Victoria Embank-ment, betwixt road and river, it was the perfect place to curl up into my coat one last time and let my exhausted mind wander. The decent began. Acid rose in my throat as my eyes closed. Bile balled in my chest and my head began to hurt like nothing I have ever experienced.

And at that point I realised that this was exactly as bad an idea as I had feared when choosing not to go through with it the last time. My massively expanded attempt at a ritual similar in design to that used for claiming a graveyard had gone horribly wrong. Because it had worked, and my mind was at the mercy of the streets.

Dream. Shamanic journeying. Overexerted imagination. What resulted could be considered any or all of those things. But for a fraction of a second I know I touched London in a way few have. I heard its wants, needs. Thousands upon thousands of voices, laughing, screaming, striving. Fucking and fighting. Pain, pleasure and potential, desire manifested through the lens of eight million lives.

The sheer weight of years crushed me beneath them as I fell inwards, becoming a dense point of light in an otherwise darkly liminal space. The noise was unbearable, but all I could do was keep trying, holding on to my request to meet the soul of the city as my very self unravelled. Unfortunately I succeeded.

It called my bluff through the voices of all its inhabitants, living and dead. A massively schizophrenic and insane hyperobject that turned a single polluted eye towards me and demanded to know who I thought I was bothering it in such a way, snarling its multilingual disgust through cracked pavement slab teeth.

Raw sewage dripped from London's mouth into waiting gutter goblin arms as it spoke, and the gremlins of rust scurried across its flesh looking for a place to hide from the ever watchful smog sylphs above them. Broken dryads swayed in time with its massively ragged breath. The whole scene would have been darkly beautiful had my mind not been reeling against the impossible scale of it all.

For the first time in my life I felt something akin to actual terror, withering under the volcanic hatred of a city that told me in no uncertain terms to both go away and stay gone. And then it was over. I jumped awake, lucid and wounded by the rebuff that I had experienced at the hands of a London that I had always thought of as a silent friend.

The acid pooled at the back of my mouth, and I dry heaved that hubris into the Thames, barely making it to the edge of the Embankment before losing control of my stomach. The journey back to the East End seemed to take forever, the Tube network now holding magickal associations for me that caused every bump and clang to carry undue significance. I ended up spending most of the next week in bed.

In hindsight the mistake was a simple one. I thought I was special. Important even. A virus flowing through the very veins of the city, able to leverage my magick to traverse its cartilage and bone, becoming one with an impossibly vast nervous system that viewed me as less than an inconsequential parasite among so many others.

The soul of London, as crazed and fragmented as it was, really did not care about me. Uncompromising and infested by the eight million points of sentience that crawled like fleas over its pavements and nested in its very bones, not to mention the uncountable dead rotting beneath, there was no compassion for the individuals who lived there. It had nothing more to give.

My question was answered, then. I left shortly after, moved across the country and avoid going back to London even now unless I have no choice. None of those visits could be considered pleasant, my skin tingling with cold fire and stale sweat for the entire duration. Paranoia sets in early, and sits on my shoulders like an unwelcome cloak.

When I need to be there for a longer period the nightmares make it impossible to sleep, swirling hatred leaving me permanently exhausted. Just like old times, yet even more draining now I know the truth. Some secrets are indeed better left to fester beneath those well worn pavements, as digging them up can only lead to more pain.

The once quietly comforting city does not care if I ever go back or not, of course. Despite my feelings towards the concrete and tarmac that gave solace to a much younger and arguably more naïve version of myself it never will. A super massive construct such as that cannot show empathy about anything.

The spirit of London is not bound by human emotions or morals, nor should it be I suppose. It just exists. As do I many miles away from the city of my birth now. While I am happy with the choice I made to follow the woman I will always love to the other side of the country I still occasionally find myself stopping to yearn for those simpler times, back before the ritual at Cleopatra's Needle was complete.

Afterword

And there is is. The Accelerated Necromancer, a book more than two decades in the making. As for me, I am but a puppet of the invisible hands that pull strings I will never see. Wants, needs, loves and loss. The souls who came before. Mine was in many ways an accident of birth that led to a life focussed upon death. A child of the void with nothing better to do than make the world a stranger place. On balance I think I succeeded.

I know things can seem dark out there, but remember that the universe you live in is a wonderful nightmare the likes of which few can face down and remain sane. Shine, my vibrant adepts. Glow like a beacon to the lost. Be the sunrise you hope to see poking over the smog choked trees. Burn hot enough to turn those in your path to ash and one day the Reaper will smile in appreciation as she takes you home.

Recommended Books

Albion, Dis, Jake Stratton-Kent, and Erzebet Carr. 2013. Conjure Codex 2.

Barthold, Erzebet, Jake Stratton-Kent, and Dis Albion. 2020. Conjure Codex 4: A Compendium of Invocation, Evocation, and Conjuration. Conjure Codex.

Berger, Helen A. 2011. *Witchcraft and Magic.* University of Pennsylvania Press.

Bis Iot. 2016. *Chaos Streams 01.* Universe Machine.

Carroll, Peter. 1987. Liber Null & Psychonaut. Red Wheel/Weiser.

Chambers, Paul. 1999. Sex and the Paranormal. Blandford Press.

Colvin, Andy, and Gray Barker. 2014. Searching for the String : Selected Writings of John A. Keel. Point Pleasant, Wv: New Saucerian Books ; Seattle.

Copenhaver, Brian P. 2015. The Book of Magic : From Antiquity to the Enlightenment. London: Penguin Books.

Finkel, I. (2021). *The First Ghosts.* Hodder & Stoughton.

Folklore, Myths and Legends of Britain. 1977. London: Reader's Digest Association.

Frater U.:D. 2012. *Practical Sigil Magic.* Llewellyn Worldwide.

Gooch, Stan. 2007. *The Origins of Psychic Phenomena.* Simon and Schuster.

Gruppo di Nun. 2023. *Revolutionary Demonology.* MIT Press.

Keel, John A. 2002. *The Mothman Prophecies.* Macmillan.

Lee, Dave. 2006. *Chaotopia! Sorcery and Ecstasy in the Fifth Aeon,* Oxford: Mandrake of Oxford.

Louv, Jason. 2006. *Generation Hex.* New York, Ny: Disinformation ; St.

Paul, Mn.

Radin, Dean I. 2018. *Real Magic : Ancient Wisdom, Modern Science, and a Guide to the Secret Power of the Universe*. New York: Harmony Books.

Rodgers, Charlotte. 2011. *The Bloody Sacrifice*. Oxford: Mandrake of Oxford.

Simon. 2008. *Necronomicon*. Lake Worth, Fl: Ibis Press ; Newburyport, Ma.

Simon (1998). *Necronomicon Spellbook*. Harper Collins.

Spence, Lewis. 1993. *Encyclopedia of Occultism*. Citadel Press.

Spencer, John, and Anne Spencer. 1992. *The Encyclopedia of Ghosts and Spirits*. London: Headline.

Wendell, Leilah. 1991. *The Necromantic Ritual Book*. New Orleans: Westgate Press.

www.ingramcontent.com/pod-product-compliance
Lightning Source LLC
Chambersburg PA
CBHW030823090426
42737CB00009B/849